Half the World

Refugees Transform the City of Trees

INVESTIGATE BOISE COMMUNITY RESEARCH SERIES
BOISE STATE UNIVERSITY
2017

VOL. 8

The Investigate Boise Community Research Series publishes fact-based essays of popular scholarship concerning the problems and values that shape metropolitan growth.

VOL. 1:
Making Livable Places: Transportation, Preservation, and the Limits of Growth
(2010)

VOL. 2:
Growing Closer: Density and Sprawl in the Boise Valley
(2011)

VOL. 3:
Down and Out in Ada County: Coping with the Great Recession, 2008-2012
(2012)

VOL. 4:
Local, Simple, Fresh: Sustainable Food in the Boise Valley
(2013)

VOL. 5:
Becoming Basque: Ethnic Heritage on Boise's Grove Street
(2014)

VOL. 6:
River by Design: Essays on the Boise River, 1915-2015
(2015)

VOL. 7:
The Other Idahoans: Forgotten Stories of the Boise Valley
(2016)

VOL. 8:
Half the World: Refugees Transform the City of Trees
(2017)

Todd Shallat, *editor*

Kathleen Rubinow Hodges, *associate editor*

Errol D. Jones, *academic editor*

Laura Winslow, *assistant editor*

Toni Rome, *graphic designer*

BOISE STATE UNIVERSITY
School of Public Service
Boise ID 83725
schoolofpublicservice@boisestate.edu

180 N. 8th St., Boise ID 83702
(208) 376-4229
To order, contact Rediscovered Books at www.rdbooks.org.

Displaced people from nearly half the world are rebuilding their lives in Boise, Idaho, "The City of Trees." Frontispiece: a Syrian girl in Turkish refugee camp waits for asylum. Opposite: Siyad from Kenya, one of Boise's top high school distance runners. Next: Sumay from the Sudan, Twin Falls refugee resettlement center; Congolese refugees.

Generous support was provided by the Patricia Herman Fund and Professor Emeritus Errol D. Jones.

ISBN: 978-0-9988909-0-6

creative commons

2017

Contents

	Foreword 8	
1	Improbable Sanctuary 10	
	The city of Boise defies red-state stereotypes. *Todd Shallat*	
2	Across the Pacific 26	
	Vietnamese, displaced by war, plant roots in the City of Trees. *Kathleen Rubinow Hodges*	
3	Chosen to Survive 46	
	A Bosnian, cut down by shrapnel, sees his life as a miracle. *Refik Sadikovic with Kathleen Rubinow Hodges*	
	Verse: *Living Witness* by Fidel Mwendambali Nshombo 68	
4	Leave One to Remember 70	
	A child's name bears witness to his mother's Rwandan struggle. *Laura Winslow*	
5	Food of the Pharaohs 80	
	Tiny teff, grown in Idaho, helps preserve Ethiopian heritage. *Emily Fritchman*	
	Gallery: *World Refugee Day* 86	
6	Nations United 96	
	Kids from many countries build one strong team. *Katherine Jones*	
7	Policing Softly 118	
	Boise police nurture community. *Chelsee Boehm*	
	Verse: *Blue* by Ruby McCarter and Daniah Kadhim 128	
8	Hidden, Silent, Confused 130	
	A survivor negotiates Boise and adolescence. *Belma Sadikovic with Todd Shallat*	
9	A Wider Perspective 138	
	Three lives – Eritrean, Bhutanese, and Afghan – help Boise see itself. *Aileen Hale with Kathleen Rubinow Hodges*	
	Verse: *Always Home* by Zoey Hills and Paw Kee Lar 152	
10	A Matter of Trust 154	
	Teachers help refugees cope. *Kathleen Mullen*	
	Epilogue 172	
	Hysteria challenges a city's commitment to human rights. *Errol D. Jones*	
	Credits and Sources 179	

Foreword

Today the number of world refugees is the highest ever recorded. The United Nations High Commissioner for Refugees counts 65.3 million uprooted people in flight from persecution and war. Few escape the squalor of border encampments, and fewer still – less than half of one percent – advance through the multiyear process for resettlement in the United States. But that fraction looms disproportionately large in the rising American furor over the politics of forced migration. No amount of testing and screening, say critics, can root out the coming jihad.

Boise, Idaho, offers a calmer perspective. Here at the base of the Rocky Mountains, in one of the whitest of American places in one of the reddest American states, 13,000 refugees from at least 53 countries are rebuilding their lives. *Half the World*, herein, samples their transformative stories. A book of history, reporting, poetry, and memoir, the collection queries how communities cope with the shock of forced migration and how strangers among us confront the foreign and unfamiliar by helping others find the best in themselves.

Todd Shallat, Ph.D.
Boise State University School of Public Affairs
March 2017

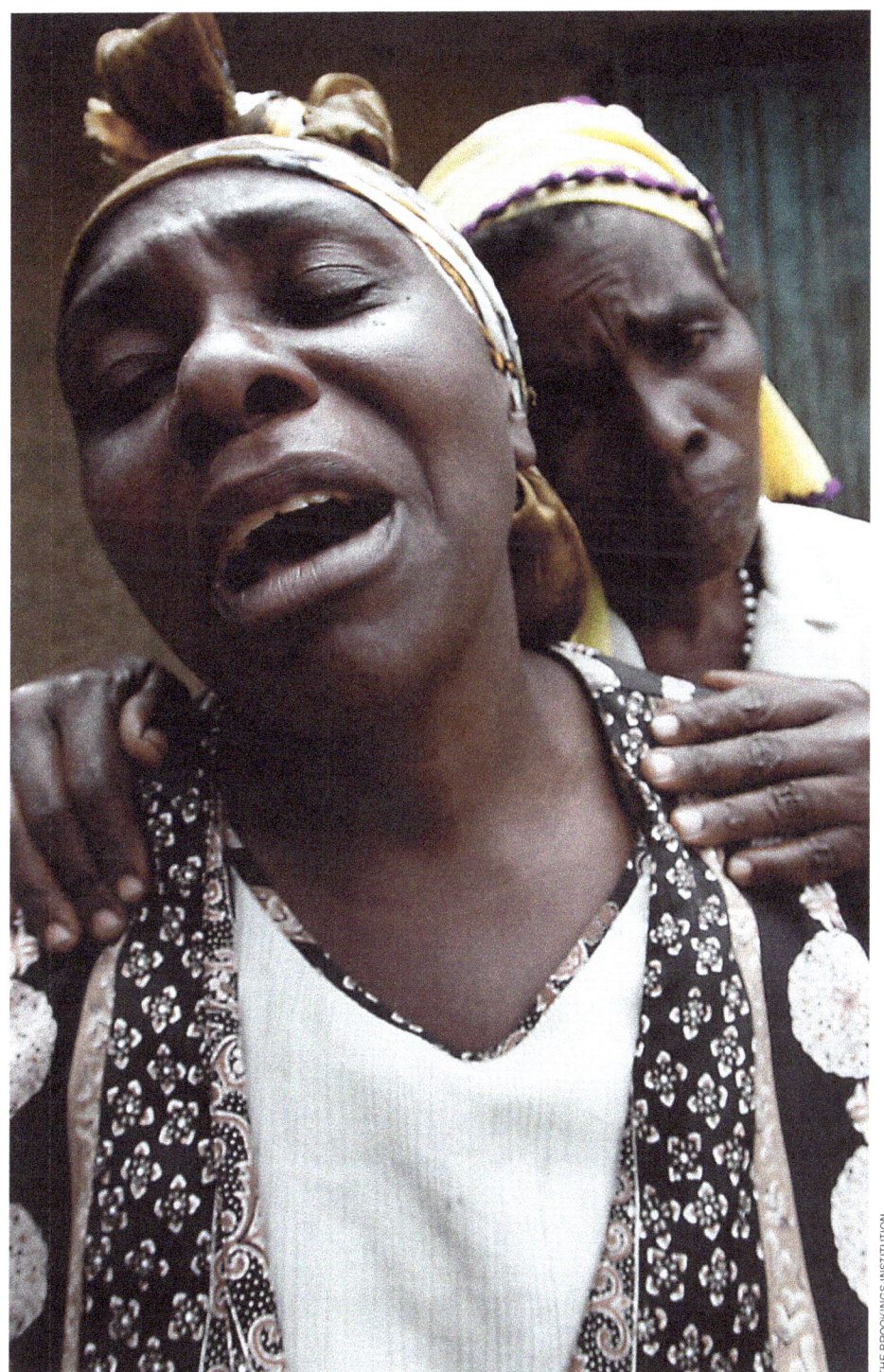

1 | Improbable Sanctuary

The city of Boise defies red-state stereotypes.

By Todd Shallat

A 60-foot cross of steel stabs a sandstone mesa. Dry wind from the sagebrush prairie flaps a 50-foot American flag. Below in the cheatgrass valley is a city known mostly for French fries. Too small potatoes for CNN election polling, too casual for Neiman Marcus, Boise, Idaho, sprawls under the radar. The daily newspaper feeds a running joke about mix-ups between Idaho (potatoes) and Iowa (corn). Tom Brokaw of NBC News once aired a Boise segment mislabeled "Des Moines."

In Boise, nevertheless, one out of every 16 people has been forced across an international border in flight from persecution and war. Thirteen thousand arrived as "displaced persons" with refugee status. Hailing from the Balkans, the Congo, the Himalayas, the Tigris-Euphrates, and the Horn of Africa, crossing oceans of suspicion and misunderstanding, they reach Idaho's capital city at a pace of about 800 people a year.

Asmaa Albukaie of Syria reached Boise via Jordan and Egypt. Married at age 14 and the mother of two at 15, she had attended university library school before the car bombs blasted Damascus. Rockets exploded with chemical sarin warheads. She hid in a basement with neighbors. Her husband and children were kidnapped. Retrieving her children, she fled.

"I force[d] to leave [be]cause my children," Albukaie told a reporter. "We couldn't sleep because of the shooting and bombs."

Across Jordan by bus and ferry, harassed, pickpocketed and swindled, the fatherless family of three eventually reached the United Nations in Cairo. Two years of vetting followed. Interrogations in windowless rooms – at least 10 that she remembers – seemed fixated on her headscarf as if her hair were hiding a bomb. Interpol, U.S. Homeland Security, the U.S. State Department, the Federal Bureau of Investigation, U.S. Customs, and the TSA all layered the cumbersome process. At last in December 2014, deemed "vulnerable" and prioritized because of the children, Albukaie and her sons were approved. The final stack of papers revealed that her family's destination was a city

seldom mentioned in Hollywood movies. She Googled the place in the airport. Inexplicably, the tickets read "Boise, ID."

"So green. It's beautiful," said Albukaie of her mystery city. In July 2016, posing for a story in the *Idaho Statesman*, she wore western denim with a a flower-print T-shirt and a hijab of bright magenta. Bright eyes flashed toward the sun.

"I have a lot of nice [Boise] friends. I'm working. I'm safe." Even so, people have cursed her in public. Drivers yelled ugly words when her clunker stalled in an intersection. A Boise woman, wide-eyed, turned to her companion and whispered "The Muslims are coming," when Albukaie entered a bank.

"[People] are talking about how we are stranger[s] … how we are ISIS." The hysteria has frightened her children and left an indelible mark. "I'm here for safety. I'm not scared. I still believe in the United States. But everyone know[s] I am Muslim if they saw me. I am a woman who wears a scarf."

Shouting Distance

Albukaie stays resolute in the face of accusations that Syrians are Muslim fanatics and that hate is the soul of Islam. "A Trojan Horse of ISIS" was how Donald Trump characterized the Syrian resettlement program. "Creeping Sharia" was the slur preferred by Idahoans who sponsored a bill to de-Islamize the state's child welfare system. In downtown Boise, a Nampa man was arrested and charged with a hate crime for punching Albukaie's 16-year-old son. The assailant had asked the boy if he was Muslim.

"Maybe it's our problem," Albukaie concedes. "Maybe we don't know how to deal with American people. I'm trying just to fix and solve the problem because I need peace for this country. For me, America is now my country, so I need peace too. So I need to be safe with my kids, and I need safety for my neighbors, for American people."

Peace and safety seemed doomed in the wake of the 2015 terror attacks on Paris and San Bernardino. In Filer, Idaho, a pastor packed a small Baptist church to preach against the "Muslim refugee agenda." Boise, said the pastor, was a "refugee dump." In Twin Falls, meanwhile, hijabs had been spotted near the College of Southern Idaho campus at the refugee

Support for refugees at the Idaho Statehouse, 2015.

Previous page: Asmaa Albukaie was among the first Syrian refugees in Boise, arriving in 2014.

Petitioning against resettlement in Twin Falls, 2016.

Twin Falls prosecutors say alleged rape by refugees never happened, 2016.

resettlement center. A news report claimed that Syrians had videotaped the gang-rape of a disabled 5-year-old child at knifepoint. Twin Falls police quickly denied it: no Syrians, no rape, no knife. All that the prosecutor would acknowledge was that "juveniles" had been involved in an "incident." The court records were sealed. Immediately, nevertheless, *Breitbart News* reposted the story. In a flash, the fiction went viral.

Governor C.L. "Butch" Otter saw the firestorm coming. Already Idaho's governor had joined two dozen others in demanding a halt to "rubber-stamped" immigration-refugee programs. No matter the confusion between refugees (who are forced to migrate) and immigrants (who are not). No matter that refugee issues were far removed from the governor's jurisdiction. "Frustration runs high in Idaho," said Otter. The narrative seemed to confirm that strangers were evil and that refugee resettlement was a top spun out of control.

Two blocks from Otter's Statehouse – shouting distance but political light-years from the governor's office – Mayor David H. Bieter ignited his own fiery headline by drafting a defiant response. "When it comes to immigration and refugees," wrote Bieter to his fellow mayors, "presidents and Congress get to say, but mayors have to do."

Mayor David H. Bieter

U.S. Senator William Borah

Boise's mayor rejected the notion that people from distant places posed a threat to public safety. Boise was live-and-let-live, said Bieter. It was the kind of place where artists painted the utility boxes, where an overpass sheltered a skate park, where motorists allowed people to merge so long as they waved back to acknowledge the kindness. "We're nationally known as a welcoming city," Bieter continued. "We can all be proud."

Pride in the welcoming city had become a rallying point for the four-term incumbent in Boise's previous mayoral election. Himself an outsider looking in – a Catholic in a Protestant city, a Democrat in a Republican state – Hizzoner embodied the broad-brush American epic of the grandson who wants to remember what the father would rather forget. His maternal grandfather, a sheepherder, had emigrated from the Basque region of Spain. Threadbare and persevering, the immigrant had taken a job few people wanted, making a life. The sheepherder's daughters had been married in the Catholic cathedral that marked the Democratic home base of the future mayor. In 2015, during Bieter's fourth mayoral campaign, his challenger had scorned "too many dialects" in Boise and refugees as "blight." The mayor coldly responded that "diversity" was Boise's birthright. Bieter then cruised to an electoral landslide with 69% of the vote.

Both an immigrant city and an anti-immigrant city, Boise, historically, had shunned prejudice but also endorsed it depending on what was at stake. In 1893, the Japanese laborers who laid rails to the 10th Street depot were confined to shiver in box cars when threatened by mobs downtown. In 1901, a Bavarian immigrant mayor named Moses Alexander allied with a British sheriff to roughly remove the Chinese. That same immigrant built an ornate synagogue and became the nation's first elected Jewish governor. Boise beckoned, but Boiseans sometimes repelled.

Pitchfork nativism, even so, never played well in Boise. In 1924, when the Knights of the Ku Klux Klan rallied on Boise's Main Street, city council insisted that the hooded marchers expose their faces in honest daylight. In 1948, when an Idaho senator shunned "whites only" and was arrested in Alabama, Boiseans applauded the rebuke of Jim Crow.

War refugees flee Berlin, 1945.

Concern for war refugees first appeared in the *Idaho Statesman* in opposition to U.S. Senator William Borah. The square-jawed attorney from Boise had risen to national stature as the prosecutor of radical labor bosses. In the 1920s, he lent a shoulder to barring the door to "undesirables" from Asia and Mexico who, he alleged, could not be assimilated. An isolationist, Borah opposed asylum for Germany's Jews. After Borah's death and the Nazi slaughter, the refugee issue resurfaced in the problem of Europe's "displaced persons" whose homes had been bombed into graveyards. President Harry Truman, in 1948, had signed the Displaced Persons Act "with very great reluctance" because the legislation discriminated against Catholics and Jews. Boise philanthropist Leo J. Falk and others supported Truman, advocated asylum, and funded resettlement programs. In 1951 the *Statesman* polled Boiseans to ask whether the United States should do more.

Protesting the U.S. refugee ban, 1938.

"If we can help, it is our duty to do it," said Phyllis Vanderwilt of Rose Hill, responding to the *Statesman's* query. Betty Horn of Eagle agreed but cautioned that there needed to be a quota. Likewise, Arleta Vanderford, a Kuna housewife, did not want America "flooded" but noted that many Holocaust survivors were good people and "highly educated." Idaho might benefit from their skills.

Owing to a Well-Founded Fear

In 1951, as Boiseans pondered asylum, a landmark United Nations treaty codified the word "refugee" in international law. Signed in Geneva, grandfathered into U.S. federal statue by Congress in 1967, the Convention on the Status of Refugees established the principle that no innocent person should be remanded to face torture or execution. A "refugee" was defined as any person forced to migrate "owing to a well-founded fear of being persecuted for reasons of race, religion, nationality, membership of a particular social group, or political opinion."

Cubans fleeing Castro in 1960 were among the first in the United States with official refugee status. Hungarians, Czechoslovakians, Russians, and Ukrainians followed as Congress cracked open the door for dissidents from the Soviet bloc. In 1975, with the fall of Saigon, Congress authorized two years' worth of funds for people fleeing Cambodia and Vietnam. However, Indochinese continued to arrive, and by midyear 1979 some 14,000 were reaching the United States each month. Members of Congress criticized U.S. refugee policy as "haphazard and inadequate ... outdated, unrealistic, and discriminatory." The Refugee Act of 1980, signed by President Carter on March 17, set up a permanent and systematic procedure for admitting refugees and an Office of Refugee Resettlement within the Department of Health and Human Services.

Vietnamese refugee, 1975

In Idaho, meanwhile, an informal refugee program began at Boise State University in 1975, and Governor John Evans formally established a state-level refugee center in 1979. The program later passed to Idaho's Department of Health and Welfare and, in 1997, to a private nonprofit. The nonprofit, named Jannus, Inc. in tribute to the Roman god of new beginnings, houses the resettlement agency. The Idaho Office for Refugees, within Jannus, receives federal grant money and administers statewide programs.

Jan Reeves, 71, the longtime director of the state's refugee office, leans back from piles of printouts in the Jannus building behind a North End strip mall. "We have a receptive community," says Reeves in response to the question of why refugees come to Boise. "We have resources. There are opportunities here. There are many community partners that are engaged in the resettlement process. Refugees have an opportunity here to start their lives over on a solid footing with a positive future ahead of them. And that's what we want."

Boiseans extend hands and open their hearts through soccer leagues, churches, and charitable foundations. A clearinghouse called Neighbors United links 16 government offices and 30 nonprofits. The Agency for New Americans provides case workers fluent in 12 languages. The International Rescue Committee has worked tirelessly to help refugees become self-sustaining. The Boise School District coordinates translation services in 84 languages. Global Talent, a Jannus affiliate, smooths the path to employment for skilled professionals. Global Gardens helps Somali Bantu farmers plant community roots.

Refugee farmer with cherry tomatoes, Global Gardens, Boise.

Welcome the Stranger

Boise's embrace is proof that right and left, secular and religious, can share common goals for different political reasons. Secular pluralism can fuse with the evangelical's sense of service when people of every stripe yearn to connect with the world. Cole Community Church, a humanitarian pioneer, rises above denomination with a family mentoring service. Mentors meet families once a week to teach the Boise basics: how to shop, pay bills, barbecue, and bike to the zoo. Annually the church sponsors an ecumenical "peace feast." Half the guest list is Muslim. Lamb killed by hand is blessed and prepared according to Islamic halal practices.

Marla Olsen of Boise credits this church at Maple Grove and Ustick as the model for programs she coordinates for eight congregations of Latter-day Saints. When it comes to service, says Olsen, "we are not Mormon or Catholic or Jewish. We're

Congolese refugee Bahati Sudjonga reunites with family at the Boise airport, 2017.

all just trying to fill in the gaps." Recently she encountered a rabbi while tutoring a refugee in a classroom provided by Boise's Temple Beth Israel. "Here," said the rabbi, smiling, "we have a Mormon in a Jewish synagogue teaching English to a Muslim."

The teaching goes two ways, says Donald Batubenga, the Congolese pastor of New Heart Christian Church. "They [the refugees] have shifted the social life of this community." Batubenga alternates sermons in English and Swahili. His parishioners are Zambian, Sudanese, Ethiopian, Nigerian, Rwandan, Caribbean, and Idahoan. Church music plays in Lingala, Bemba, Zulu, Creole, English, and French.

"Red or blue, victory or not, we need each other," said Rev. Sara LaWall, a Boise Unitarian. Her voice was strong in December 2015 at a rain-soaked vigil on the stairs of the Idaho Statehouse. Singing "This Land Is Your Land" and waving bike lights and glow sticks, there was no mistaking the political message. "Faith calls us to value love over fear," said LaWall. "All of our faith teachings have strong support of refugees."

Boiseans sang even louder in outrage over President Trump's pledge to ban Syrian refugees and suspend immigration from majority-Muslim countries. On January 29, a rally of more than 600 crowded the Boise airport. Placards

read "Love Trumps Hate," "United We Stand," and "Fight Ignorance." A teenager held a sign that said, "We Love Our Muslim Neighbors." Another implored "Don't Take Our 1st Amendment." A girl in pink knelt on the carpet in a throng of children with a "Welcome Refugees" sign.

At Boise City Council, meanwhile, a solidarity resolution reaffirmed "a responsibility to welcome, speak up for, and stand with all of our residents regardless of where they are from." Two days later, again at the Boise airport, a crowd of 100 tearfully cheered Bahati Sudjonga as he stepped through the gate to reunite with his brother and sister. The Congolese refugee, age 19, said his name means "lucky one" in Swahili. He was said to have been "the last refugee" to reach Boise before the President's ban.

That "last refugee" waves an American flag in a jubilant photo posted by the *Wall Street Journal*. Reposted by Boise's Neighbors United, it flanks profiles of refugees whose heritage the President shuns. One is a young Somali medical doctor. Threatened by jihadists, he had been a student at the top of his class before fleeing to seek safety in Jordan. Another profiled refugee is an Afghan student at Boise State. Her father is a well-known poet; her mother, a literature professor. The family had fled the Taliban, escaped to Uzbekistan, and there waited 15 years for third-country asylum. "In America," she still believes, "freedom offers unlimited opportunities." Whether Trump's America will stand by that promise is an open question as this book goes to press.

Top Three Countries of Origin for Idaho Refugees, 2016

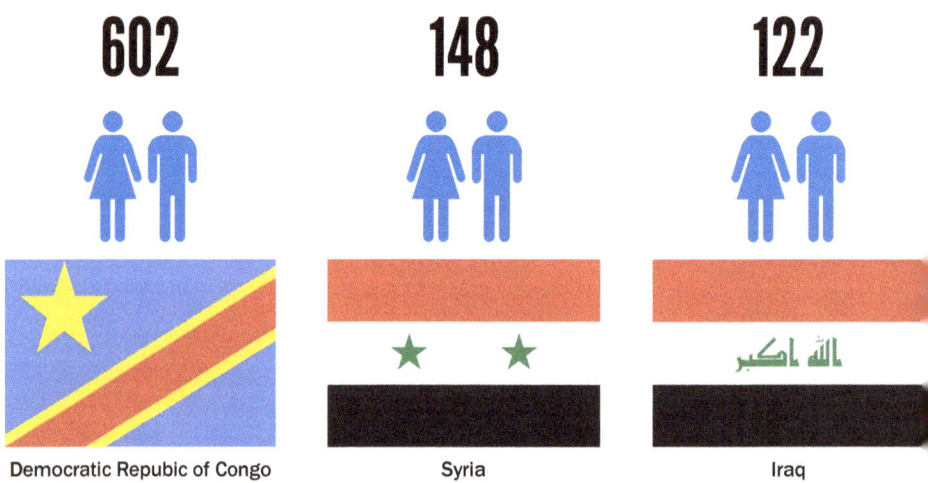

By the Numbers

In 2016, the Idaho Office for Refugees oversaw the resettlement of 1,245 displaced people. Two-thirds were resettled in Boise, the rest in Twin Falls. The single largest group was 602 refugees from the Democratic Republic of

Congo (former Zaire). Next in numbers were Syrians (148) and Iraqis (122). The numbers suggest that most will build lives in the Boise area. Since 1975, of an estimated 24,500 refugees and asylum-seekers who have reached Idaho through various channels, about 19,000 remain.

But in Idaho, as in the rest of America, mythology clouds the process. One pervasive fiction is that the United States does not have the bureaucratic capacity to adequately vet refugees from war zones. Security experts say otherwise. America's refugee screening process has been called the most arduous ever invented. In 2016, in testimony before the U.S. Senate's immigration subcommittee, Homeland Security's Leon Rodriguez said there was no harder way to enter the country than as a refugee. "All refugees," he insisted, "are subject to the highest level of security check of any category of any traveler to the United States." Homeland Security could confirm "not a single act of terrorist violence" committed by a screened refugee.

A second fiction is that refugees bleed the coffers of public assistance. Taxpayer support, in fact, is a pittance once refugees land. A family of four in Boise might get $782/month for up to eight months. Refugees have 40 months to repay the cost of their flight to freedom. Refugees, like any American, immediately pay state and federal taxes, and, like any American, the poorest among them pay the highest percentage of their household income. In 2016, in response to a public petition, the Twin Falls school superintendent tallied the annual cost of refugee services. The total annual cost to the school budget was less than half of one percent.

"If refugees weren't self-sufficient, that would be a problem, but that's not what's happening," said Zeze Rwasama, who directs the College of Southern Idaho's refugee center.

A third, more complex, fiction is the notion that refugees displace other workers. In the short run, if the Boise Valley were a zero-growth economy of stagnation, it could be argued that any influx of workers would devastate wages. But studies of the long run have shown that refugees in agricultural regions can reduce the dependence on guest or undocumented

Refugee Arrivals in Idaho

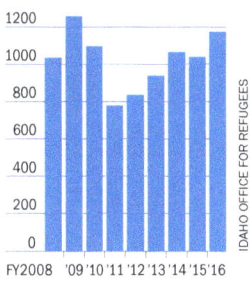

A family of four in Boise might get $782/month for up to eight months. Refugees have 40 months to repay the cost of their flight to freedom.

workers by filling undesirable jobs. Some start businesses that employ other people. Refugees are also consumers. Less likely than other immigrants to leave once established, they are "integral to the nation's growth" according to a panel of 14 academic economists in their 2016 report to the National Academies of Sciences, Engineering, and Medicine. "We found little to no negative effects on overall wages and employment of native-born workers in the longer term," said Francine D. Blau of Cornell, who led the study.

Boise restaurateurs Salam and Aseel Bunyan, refugees from Iraq via Syria, 2016.

Entrepreneurship is also important. A 2016 report from the Center for American Progress found that Bosnians, after ten years in the workforce, were about as likely to open a business as the American born. Thirty-one of every 1,000 Bosnians had become business owners; so had 26 of every 1,000 Burmese and 26 of every 1,000 Somalis. The Syrian-born, who are typically skilled and well-educated, were three times more likely to open a viable business than the American-born. The study cautioned, however, that refugee success was as varied as their ethnicities and education. Bosnians and Burmese exceeded American rates of home ownership. Somalis did not.

The Idaho Office for Refugees counts more than 300 businesses started by people resettled in Boise. "When you open a business for the first time in the United States, that's not something easy," says Salam Bunyan, a chef who hails from Iraq. Bunyan and his wife, Aseel, are proud to

Chobani CEO Hamdi Ulukaya employs refugee workers at his yogurt plant in Twin Falls.

employ American workers. So is Tino Silva of Meridian's Intermountain Construction and Abatement. A Zions Bank small business loan helped Silva rebuild the struggling business, keeping nine Idahoans employed.

"This economic impact flows directly into cities like Boise," says Nikki Cicerani of Upwardly Global, a nonprofit employment service. More than half of Cicerani's refugee clients are skilled professionals who prosper in fields like

Personal Contact with Refugees, Idaho Public Opinion Survey, 2017

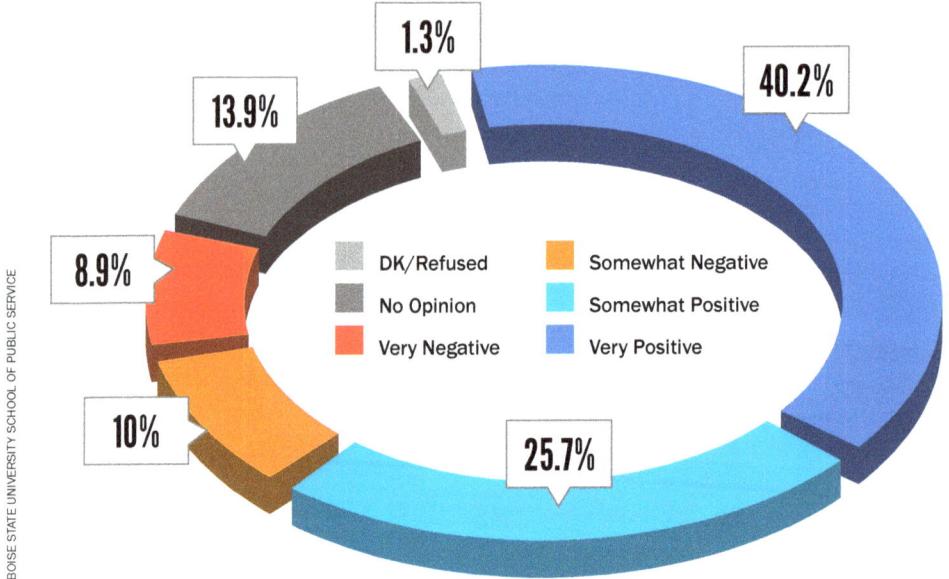

engineering, IT, and finance. "To view refugees as outsiders, victims, or a danger to their communities," says Cicerani, "is a narrow and inaccurate lens."

Certainly not everyone prospers in Boise. Refugees, for all their resilience, face the same economy as other Boiseans seeking employment – an economy of call centers and baristas, a city with too few apartments close to a job or a bus stop. Idaho suffers from the nation's highest percentage of employment at minimum wage. And that minimum is $2.50 less than the minimum an hour away across the Oregon line. Fifteen percent of people in the Boise Valley live in poverty by federal standards. Another 22 percent are so-called ALICE workers (Asset-Limited, Income-Constrained, Employed) who earn less than the minimum needed for housing, groceries, and health care.

Transportation is another problem. The federal transit administration has ranked Boise at 251 out of 290 cities for public transportation. For people who spent years in camps without cars or driver's licenses, that statistic is especially tough.

"You know, new country is supposed to be hard," says Nowela Virginie of Boise by way of Rwanda. The mother of two, age 23, she spent 16 years in a Tanzanian refugee camp. Virginie reached Boise in 2009 at the nadir of the Great Recession, when employment for the newly arrived had dipped to 55 percent. She has since found work as a maid in a Boise motel.

"If you have a job, you have education, is not hard. Is good," says Virginie. "But the bad thing, if you don't speak any English, is so hard – really hard."

It's no wonder Idahoans seem to be all over the map on refugee resettlement issues. In 2016, in a Boise State University poll of 1,000 Idahoans, a statewide plurality (48.8 percent) thought that refugees burdened the local economy. But the poll also suggested that familiarity bred respect. Among respondents who had contact with refugees, a sizable majority (66 percent) had positive experiences. The more people knew about refugees, the better they were perceived.

"They're going to provide such richness to our way of life," says Luke Carter of Boise, a refugee mentor who was recently featured on the mayor's website. Carter and Sally, his wife, feel "humbled" to have befriended a hard-working family from Burma. "Basically, we're family. We all fit together. They want to be good Americans. They want to contribute. They're here to stay."

Citizenship ceremony in Boise, 2012.

TODD SHALLAT, PH.D., teaches history and urban studies at Boise State University. He is the three-time winner of the Idaho Library Association's Idaho Book Award.

2 | Across the Pacific

Vietnamese, displaced by war, plant roots in the City of Trees.

By Kathleen Rubinow Hodges

In 1975, at the end of the Vietnam War, thousands of displaced Vietnamese sought asylum in the United States. Several hundred ended up in Idaho. Those refugees paved the way for many others. Idahoans pioneered creative and humane ways of managing the influx. Although many Vietnamese later left for other regions of the U.S., those who stayed have made Boise home.

April 30, 1975

United States' involvement with the country of Vietnam stretched over several decades, gradually escalating from support of the French colonial regime after World War II to a full-on war against the Communist north in the 1960s. By 1973, the American public had had enough, and President Nixon pulled out U.S. troops. However, civil war between North and South Vietnam continued for two more years. In March 1975, the Communists defeated southern armies at Ban Me Thuot in the Central Highlands and advanced rapidly as southern soldiers and ordinary citizens fled. The quick collapse of southern defenses left many suddenly scrambling to escape. The frantic exodus included the last Americans (advisers, embassy workers, and contractors), their Vietnamese dependents, and members of the South Vietnamese government and military. On April 30, the South officially surrendered and the last helicopter left the roof of the United States embassy.

Among the Vietnamese trying desperately to leave were some future Boise residents. On April 30, 1975, Hung Van Tran was a 20-year-old soldier in South Vietnam's air force. His unit had been stationed in a new area south of Saigon City for just a few weeks. As victorious Communist soldiers marched through Saigon City, Tran, young and frightened, had to decide what to do. In an interview 15 years later, he explained his predicament.

The men at his base were given a choice by their commander: they could stay and fight to the last bullet, or they could go home to their families. Tran decided to go to his mother's house in Saigon. He got on a bus, but after a few miles it stopped because the

ACROSS THE PACIFIC

Uniforms abandoned by South Vietnamese soldiers, 1975.

Previous page: U.S. sailors rescue refugees from a barge in the South China Sea, 1975.

Helicopter pushed over the side of USS Okinawa to clear the deck for more refugees, 1975.

roads were blocked. He became separated from his friends, and not knowing what else to do, he returned to the place where his unit had been stationed. He said: "I go back to my barrack, everybody gone. There was a panic over there. The people, they come inside the air force to pick up anything the soldiers left over. So I didn't know who was Communist, because they be dressed the same, you know, and here I in the uniform. It was scary. So I went back to my room to find my clothes in there. Gone! And when I left, I just carried one pair of clothes I can have with me. So what I did was I changed in there, and I throw my uniform away. I was really panicked. In my uniform was my wallet. All the papers carried with me in the uniform. And I walk about half an hour, and I say, 'Where is my wallet?' I went back and gone. So I lost – I was there in a panic area without paperwork. I didn't know where to go. So I went around and I didn't know what to do, but I know one thing in my mind was if the Communists catch me, I rather kill myself because I can't survive."

Hung Van Tran managed to get into a helicopter and ended up with other refugees on the aircraft carrier USS Midway. So many helicopters were trying to land on U.S. carriers out in the South China Sea that many of them were pushed off into the ocean to make room for more. In that atmosphere of panic, Tran was given the opportunity to go to the United States. He accepted because he believed that his sister had also fled to the United States, and he wanted to find her. He was taken to Guam and from there to Camp Pendleton in California.

Another future Boisean, Kim-Phung Hoang, was 8 years old in 1975. She crossed the Pacific to Guam on an overcrowded Vietnamese-operated ship. Her entire family had planned to come to the United States, but at the last minute her mother became sick and had to stay behind. That left the father, formerly a proud career man in the South Vietnamese navy, with the responsibility of caring for six small children. On board ship, he had to beg for food.

Still another man tried to bring his savings with him, but there was a run on his Saigon bank. Loc Nguyen tried to cash his last paycheck, but could only change it for $20 in United

States currency. He said: "I didn't know. I thought maybe that was a lot of money in the United States." When he and his wife left from Tan Son Nhut Airport in Saigon, she carried their baby daughter and Nguyen carried an armful of diapers and canned formula.

Nearly 20,000 refugees were relocated to Camp Pendleton in 1975.

Refugees, however they managed to leave Vietnam, ended up first in a temporary camp set up on Guam and then in one of four reception centers on the United States mainland: Camp Pendleton, California; Fort Chaffee, Arkansas; Eglin Air Force Base, California; or Fort Indiantown Gap, Pennsylvania. In order to leave the camps, refugees had to be sponsored by an individual, a family, or an organization like a church. Sponsors agreed to take responsibility until refugees got on their feet. In order to alleviate pressure on any one community or state, sponsorships were deliberately set up all around the United States. After a stay on Guam, the Hoang family was sponsored by an individual in Caldwell. Loc Nguyen and his wife were fortunate because they were able to arrange a sponsorship in California through their church, the Seventh-day Adventists.

Vietnamese refugees arrive at the Boise airport, 1975.

(He got a job with Pacific Press, the publishing arm of the church, which several years later opened a branch in Nampa, Idaho, at which point the Nguyens moved here.) Hung Van Tran was sent to Texas, but a year later, he met some friends from Camp Pendleton who had been living in Idaho. "They say, 'You want to see real snow? Come to Idaho.' I say, 'What the heck, to me it doesn't matter where I go.'" And so he also ended up in Boise.

As the war ended, public reaction in Boise, Idaho, was a mixture of relief and anger. The pages of the *Idaho Statesman* reflected a debate. In the first weeks of April, some Idahoans wrote letters to the editor: "I would have used nuclear bombs and made a Grand Canyon out of that Ho Chi Minh Trail." "If the United States would have squished the Communists like a spider the first moment we became involved in the Vietnam situation, hundreds of thousands would be alive today." However, newspaper articles also quoted people who were willing to be done with the war. "We've finished over there. We shouldn't start again. We have our own problems, our own people to look after." "After all this time, I'm relieved … to have an end to the whole thing – the bloodshed, the plunder of the land and the people." A Vietnam veteran expressed bitterness: "I don't think we accomplished anything over there. It was all a waste of lives and money."

Some Idahoans, including Governor Cecil Andrus, were reluctant to accept refugees, saying Idaho should "help its own first," but others welcomed them, mostly for altruistic reasons (though one man hoped the refugees could move irrigation pipe). Official numbers are hard to come by for 1975 to 1977, but a substantial number of individuals and churches volunteered to sponsor refugees. In August 1975, an *Idaho Statesman* article estimated about 50 refugees had arrived but also quoted the U.S. Immigration and Naturalization Service, which gave a figure of 65. Later the newspaper quoted Pastor Van Hoogan of the Christian Missionary Alliance who thought perhaps 200 Vietnamese people lived in Boise. The Boise School District had 46 Vietnamese students in September 1975 and more by December of that year.

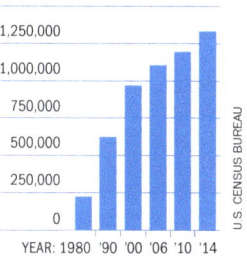

Vietnamese Immigrant Population in the United States, 1980-2014

Services Established

The first organized efforts to help refugees in Idaho on more than an individual basis began almost by accident. Helen Huff was director of adult education at Boise State University. One late night in May 1975, she was alone at the Adult Learning Center catching up on paperwork. She heard a knock on the door and opened it to find a group of refugees with their sponsors. Quickly, she phoned her husband who brought some neighbors to help serve tea and coffee, and a refugee program was born. English classes began in July. The program, though it eventually channeled state and federal money, was run as part of BSU until 1983. According to Huff (interviewed in 1990), Idaho was the only state where refugee resettlement was set up as part of an educational institution.

Huff explained that the program provided people with tools to become self-sufficient and independent. From the beginning, it had a practical focus and made heavy use of volunteers. Refugees and other adult learners studied "survival English," focusing on the vocabulary needed in daily living. Staff encouraged the refugees to find employment as quickly as possible. Employees and volunteers followed newly hired refugees to job sites, wrote down relevant vocabulary, and then taught the words and phrases to their students. When a Vietnamese woman bought a car and drove it through a fence, a gate, and a garage door, the refugee program developed driver education classes. Huff worked with the Department of Transportation, finding someone to translate the Idaho driver's

Vietnamese children learn basic English.

Idaho's refugee center at Boise State University, 1975.

manual into Vietnamese so she could use it as a training tool in English classes. She recruited George Nakano, a high school teacher, to serve as driving instructor.

In her interview in 1990, she emphasized that her program kept a clear line of separation from any religious influences, even though over the years much refugee work has been done by churches. It is true that the aforementioned Pastor Van Hoogan of the Christian Missionary Alliance helped to set up classes in 1975 when some Vietnamese members of his church moved to Boise, but it is unclear how long he was involved. In any case, Huff said that she tried for a wide community base for the newly organized Refugee Center, cooperating with various businesses in addition to state agencies. The Simplot Company hired many refugees. Retired Boise business owners Ken and Ethel Farnsworth helped with transportation and with teaching basic home economics like how to shop for groceries in American stores. A local bank allowed classes to come in and play-act all the steps of setting up an account and cashing a check.

Meanwhile, the Boise School District response to refugee students was quick and flexible. In the fall of 1975, the district put 10 elementary students in one class with a Vietnamese woman as an aide. At Boise High, refugee students attended a pull-out class for English two hours per day. By December, a Vietnamese man began work as a high school aide. Programs in the schools continued as additional refugees arrived. When the semester began, news articles about the Vietnamese students assumed that they would fit in quickly, with headlines like "Enjoy Pep Rally, Football, TV." As the months went by, school and community officials realized that resettlement was not an easy process.

Certainly, 1975 was not an easy year for the refugees. Traumatized by their flight from Vietnam, they struggled to cope with a new language, strange customs, and inhospitable weather. Many worried about family members left behind. By the end of 1975, the four refugee reception centers in the United States closed their gates. Approximately 120,000 Vietnamese refugees, plus a smaller number of Cambodians and Laotians, had resettled in various parts of the United

States. According to a Health, Education, and Welfare report submitted to Congress in June 1976, about 400 of those refugees had come to Idaho.

Boat People, 1978-1980s

Over the next two years, a few more Southeast Asians arrived at various locations in the United States assisted by several international humanitarian agencies (called "voluntary agencies," these groups aided refugees around the world). Then in 1978, numbers increased dramatically as two more groups of people fled.

Soon after assuming power over a unified Vietnam, the Communist government imprisoned men who had served

Refugees await rescue from a fishing boat 350 miles northeast of Cam Ranh Bay, 1984.

Refugees in a Malaysian camp are interviewed to determine resettlement eligibility to the United States, 1979.

as military officers and government officials for the South. In 1975, former first lieutenant Yung Ha had to report for meetings, also called "re-education." He was prevented from returning home and spent several years in prison, followed by forced labor on a farm. After five years, he escaped and bought places for himself and his son on a small boat with 32 other people. After four days, he arrived at a refugee camp in Malaysia. His wife and daughter got out on a different boat to Thailand several months later. His wife's boat broke down and traveled very slowly; Ha had a close brush with Thai pirates. Nevertheless, he described himself as "lucky" because they all survived, arriving in Boise several years later. He explained, "Nobody wants to leave your native country, but you can't live with your enemy." Many former military and government officials had similar experiences.

In addition, Vietnamese of Chinese ethnicity were persecuted by the Communist government. Many Chinese, often second or third generation in Vietnam, had owned independent businesses and saved a considerable amount of money, which the Communist government confiscated. They also left the country. In 1989, Boise State University student Ben Luu explained: "In Vietnam most of the Chinese control the economy: export, import, contracting with the government, is in the Chinese hands. In Vietnam, the Chinese don't deal with politics. Whatever government is in control, they still okay as long as their business running smooth. … But the Communists, at first they let these businesses keep going. Later on, everything shut down, everything taken into the government hands." In 1978, the government began forcing Chinese to leave Vietnam, extorting high cash payments from them in the process. Chinese people made their way to refugee camps throughout Southeast Asia, where they waited for months or even years to be admitted to a third country where they could settle. Luu, as the oldest son, traveled alone to Hong Kong and then to Boise, where he began paperwork to bring the rest of his family after him.

Another Chinese Vietnamese man, Victor Quang Hang, was the fourth generation of his family to live in Vietnam, but he still retained a strong Chinese identity, having gone to Chinese language school as a youth. The government jailed his father for two years and confiscated most of the land in the family's once large and prosperous farm. In 1982, when Victor was fifteen years old, his father paid for his escape, and he walked overland through Cambodia to Thailand. He spent two and a half years in a refugee camp that he described as a jail, because as far as the Thais were concerned the refugees were illegal immigrants. Inside, the camp was inhabited by both Cambodians and Vietnamese. The United Nations and the Red Cross supplied water and small amounts of food. The camp moved as fighting ebbed and flowed across the border area during the dry season. Immigration officials came to the camp, interviewing people to decide who could come to the United States. They made Hang so nervous he forgot his own birthday. Nevertheless, he passed the interview, eventually joining a friend in Boise in 1985.

By the end of 1978, people were escaping from Vietnam by the tens of thousands. Some traveled overland across Cambodia to Thailand, more traveled by boat to Malaysia

Postage stamp from Galang Refugee Camp, home to 250,000 Vietnamese, 1979-1996.

and Hong Kong. This new exodus came to be known as the "boat people." They arrived at squalid camps in neighboring countries, which did not have the resources to take them in. Eventually, they numbered hundreds of thousands. Refugees from the political turmoil of Cambodia and Laos joined refugees from Vietnam. Like Yung Ha, Ben Luu, and Victor Quang Hang, they petitioned for admittance to the U.S. or to other countries such as Australia, Canada, and France.

Refugees wade ashore in Malaysia, 1979.

The aggregate numbers of people fleeing by small boat, drowning at sea, and existing precariously in overcrowded refugee camps horrified the world. In the summer of 1979, an international conference tried to find solutions, and U.S. President Jimmy Carter agreed to accept a large number of refugees. In March 1980, the United States passed a refugee act that put the United States definition of refugee in line with international definitions and set up a regular process, with an annual number of incoming refugees to be agreed upon by the president in consultation with Congress.

Meanwhile, the Refugee Center in Idaho had obtained some grant money through the Adult Learning Center at BSU and extended outreach programs around the state under a program called Adult Basic Education. However, most work was still done by volunteers. In August 1979, religious leaders, responding to the world situation, called for action. Governor Evans reluctantly appointed a task force (headed by Employment Department Director Glenn Nichols and Lieutenant Governor Phil Batt), which obtained a hefty federal grant from the U.S. Department of Labor. In November 1979, the state established an official Idaho Refugee Center. Continued funding, to come from U.S. Health and Welfare, would still be channeled through Boise State University with Helen Huff as the head of the agency. (The structure was convoluted – Huff was officially a Boise State employee but also reported directly to the governor.)

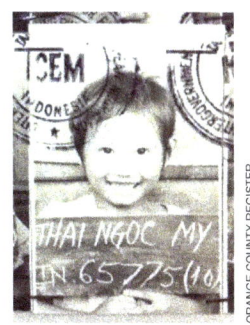

Refugee identification photo, 1977

At the international level, a new program, called Orderly Departure, or ODP, was set up by the Republic of Vietnam and the United Nations High Commissioner for Refugees (UNHCR). The government of Vietnam agreed to limit departing refugees (it had been in fact accepting bribes and therefore encouraging people to leave). In return, countries of first asylum in Southeast Asia agreed to stop pushing boats full of refugees back out to sea, and the United States and other countries around the world agreed to accept yearly quotas of refugees until the camps emptied out. In Boise, this meant that Vietnamese people here could now file paperwork to bring family members. Ben Luu, for instance, was able to bring his parents and siblings, although the process was long. He began filling out forms in 1982, and his family finally was able to fly directly to Boise seven years later, in 1989.

The Refugee Center continued to go through organizational changes over the decade of the 1980s, resulting in diminished numbers of refugee entrants in the years 1983 and 1987. In 1983, the Refugee Center moved from BSU to the Idaho Department of Health and Welfare. Helen Huff moved from the Center to head a voluntary agency called the Idaho International Institute, and then retired in 1986. Also, during the 1980s, refugees began arriving from Eastern Europe: Poles, Czechs, and Russians.

A Community Develops

In the 1980s, the number of Vietnamese and other Indochinese refugees entering Idaho trended upward. The

Boise's Orient Market on Emerald at Orchard, founded by Vietnamese refugees.

earliest arrivals began to settle in, though life was still very difficult. Many of the 1975 refugees had been professionals in Vietnam. In Idaho they suffered downward mobility, working at entry-level jobs in several trailer factories, as restaurant dishwashers, as teacher's aides, or in electronics assembly. The psychological adjustment was difficult. Son Dam, a former soldier who arrived in 1975, explained that the boat people were "already aware before they left [Vietnam], they may have some learning English background before they start. For us, we just – boom, here! And everything just, you know, just upside down, just like that. We didn't expect it, anything. And that, I think, was tougher." The boat people, as they began to arrive, had a different story that could include years of imprisonment, preparation for an escape, sometimes multiple escape attempts, and perilous situations in leaky boats and overcrowded camps. On the other hand, they had more time to get used to the idea that they would be starting different lives in new surroundings.

Son Dam and Ben Luu both said that social activities in Boise began to pick up in the 1980s. That would make sense, as more refugees arrived in those years. In fact, Luu specifically mentioned that one of the aims of social get-togethers was for the earlier residents to meet the new people, to get some information about what was going on back in Vietnam.

Over time, earlier arrivals were able to help later refugees. In 1989, Philip Dao, owner of the Orient Market, organized a Vietnamese Friendship Association. The Association met new arrivals at the airport, organized Vietnamese New Year celebrations and other parties, published a newsletter, and gave Vietnamese language lessons to Vietnamese American children. Dao got the names of Vietnamese families from the Refugee Center and added to the list by talking to customers who came into his store. The Vietnamese lessons had the goal of keeping the community's children literate in their first language.

Several groceries and restaurants helped to hold the community together. The first of these began as a grocery store, which sold imported Asian food. Opened in 1975 by Nhu Lofstedt, the business did well and moved in 1979 to larger quarters at Franklin and Curtis. Lofstedt, the wife of an American man, came to the United States shortly before 1975, so she was never technically a refugee, but her business helped to anchor the fledgling refugee community. Gradually she transitioned from groceries to casual prepared food and then to a formal restaurant. Called simply the Vietnamese Restaurant, it appealed to a clientele that was a cross-section of Boise, and it was in business for several decades. Another

Checkout at the Orient Market, 2016.

A taste of Saigon on Franklin at Curtis.

Vietnamese woman, Dao Nelson, opened a grocery store called Bien Hoa in the mid-1980s. Located on Fairview near Five Mile, the store had a clientele that included both Asian shoppers and, as her daughter put it, "American women with their cookbooks." It also had a back room where young people gathered to play French billiards and drink pop. Philip Dao opened a third store, the Orient Market. It was located at first behind a furniture store on Orchard Street and then moved to a larger space on Emerald Street. Dao, a former officer in the Army of the Republic of Vietnam, arrived in Boise in 1984. He went to work for Micron Technology but felt more comfortable going into business for himself. He chose to open a market because he thought his English was not good enough at the time to "make business with the Americans, so I just make business with the Oriental people." Dao gradually expanded, moving to a larger store space and finding wholesale suppliers who could provide the ingredients for a variety of Asian cuisines, including Chinese, Thai, Malaysian, and Indonesian cooking. He drove to Portland or San Francisco every two weeks to pick up a truckload of fresh produce. In 1988, he and his wife opened a restaurant near the market, named Nha Trang after his home town.

Vietnamese people who were not business owners found jobs in a variety of situations. Businesses that could use casual labor, such as several trailer factories in Nampa and Caldwell, hired many refugees. The Simplot Company hired during the early years. Later, in the 1980s and 1990s, many Vietnamese found work at Boise's two high-tech firms, Hewlett-Packard and Micron Technology. Both companies were expanding (though Micron went through some ups and downs due to fluctuations in the price of computer chips). Assembly jobs at both places could be performed by people with little English. People with some command of English could easily do technical work that was more numerical than verbal. Micron had a policy of hiring refugees. One Micron employee in the personnel department explained that refugees were "willing to work hard, and they like to work overtime." A Vietnamese woman confirmed that perception: "Some [Vietnamese] people, they took two jobs. Hardworking. I knew four people who worked two jobs: one at Micron, and the other job at like restaurant or whatever, too. And like the other one I know, she told me she works overtime, so almost 12 hours per day, seven days per week. So they're really hardworking people. They love their jobs." Continuing a pattern that was established in the early days with Helen Huff, Micron cooperated closely with the Refugee Center offering classes in English for employees.

Vietnamese Americans suited up for assembly lines at Hewlett-Packard and Micron.

Vietnamese people also helped each other to find jobs. Son Dam described finding his first job in Boise: "A friend had Wednesday off, and going to take me, go find a job. And meanwhile he contact with another guy who work in a trailer factory. And then, that Wednesday come and he took me to this job, and he even fill the papers for me. And I didn't even speak English that much, you know. … Usually we just help each other and make time, just drive around, drop application everywhere until you find a job. That what I used to do for friends, for people that even I don't know."

By the early 1990s, Boise's Vietnamese had gradually settled down and assimilated to some degree. Although they held on to Vietnamese customs and traditions, they learned to navigate in American society and culture. People interviewed in 1989 and 1990 were reflective and philosophical about the process. Ben Luu, who had been joined in Boise by his parents and all his brothers and sisters, did not miss much about Vietnam. He said: "I not pay attention that much about

Vietnam, you know, since my family over here. But in the past I always – anything about Vietnam I will take a second look or read about it. … I just not that much – what do you call it? Anxiety. A big relief [to have my family here]." Son Dam had a brother and sister in Boise, but his mother and sister remained in Vietnam. He felt that he had grown up in the United States. He had some bad experiences in Vietnam during the war and did not miss that aspect of his old life. "I miss the beautifulness of my country. I miss the food, miss the place I hang out." He emphasized that he felt "Americanized," which he defined as being more direct and goal-oriented. He said he looked toward the future, not the past: "I am a survivor, and I want a new thing. I don't want old things all the time. That's done, so I want something new. I'm not going to recycle it all the time."

In 1989, it was still not possible to visit Vietnam. Hung Van Tran, though working at a good job at Hewlett-Packard, married, and the father of two children, expressed a sadness that ran through his successful and respectable life, asking the interviewer: "Would you want to go to another country and have more than what you have today over here, but you never see your family again, without them, would you do it? Would you want to go to another country without knowing the language and society, their culture, would you do it? … When you're sick, you have nowhere to explain what kind of sickness you have. When you want to say something you really wanted, people could not understand you."

Fast Forward: 2017

In the early 1990s, refugees continued to come to the United States and to Boise. However, efforts to slow the rate at which people left Vietnam, coupled with international resettlement, eventually reduced the number of refugees remaining in Southeast Asian camps to a very small number. After 1997, the U.S. no longer offered refugee status to Vietnamese people. It has now been 42 years since Saigon fell and the Vietnam War ended. There has been time for a generation of Vietnamese Americans born in the United States to come to adulthood. People who arrived as children are middle-aged adults, and their parents are senior citizens.

Buddhist nun Diep Nguyen escaped Can Tho via Malaysia, reaching Boise in 1982.

Headlines about Syria recall the tragic past for Vietnamese refugees, 2015.

Since 1997, Vietnamese have continued to move to the United States, but they are immigrants – not refugees. First-generation Vietnamese in the U.S. now number around 1.3 million people.

During the past four decades, though Vietnamese in the U.S. and in Boise have struggled against enormous obstacles, they have managed to save money, buy homes, start businesses, and send their kids to college. Nationally, although employment for the group is still disproportionately skilled blue collar, there are many professionals, including engineers, artists, scholars, authors, and business people.

Vietnamese Americans are entrepreneurial, starting small businesses because of a real drive to be self-sufficient. In Boise, in addition to Vietnamese restaurants and several Asian grocery stores, there are a number of nail salons. In 1975, the actress Tippi Hedren (star of Hitchcock's movie *The Birds*) got involved in refugee relief in California. She realized that Vietnamese women needed employment. Some Vietnamese women admired Hedren's elegantly polished long nails. She got the idea to train those few women in the art of manicure, and their businesses took off. Now, half the nail salons in the U.S. are operated by Vietnamese, and Boise is no exception. A quick look at the community bulletin board at the Orient Market on Emerald Street shows multiple handwritten help wanted ads, in both English and Vietnamese, advertising for nail artists. A Vietnamese American woman, Lynde Bailey, confirmed

Most nail salons in the Boise Valley are owned by Vietnamese, an entrepreneurial tradition that began in 1975 when actress Tippi Hedren trained refugee women in the art of manicure.

that most of the nail salons in and around Boise are owned by Vietnamese.

The movement of people within the United States, from the many scattered areas where the first refugees were sent to a few areas where large communities of Vietnamese now live, has intensified. Thus, the Vietnamese population of Boise is small, probably smaller than it was in 1990, although the Vietnamese population of the United States has grown in that same amount of time. Philip Dao, the grocery store owner who arrived in Boise in 1984, has witnessed over 30 years of Vietnamese life here. In 2016, he mentioned that most Vietnamese left Boise to move to a warmer climate or to be part of one of the large Vietnamese communities that have grown up in California, Florida, and Texas. Bailey remarked that probably most Vietnamese who have remained here are connected to one of several extended families in the Treasure Valley. She said those who did not have a lot of family connections moved away. Dao and Bailey both pointed out that there is no longer the level of community ethnic identity and activity that there was 20 years ago. For instance, Vietnamese New Year is celebrated only at the family level.

Relations between the United States and Vietnam normalized in 1995. It is now possible for Americans to visit Vietnam, and many Vietnamese Americans have made the trip. The older generation visits family and friends, while younger U.S.-born millennials travel to find their roots. Dao, whose family still owns a grocery store, the Asia Market on Fairview, has been back ten times. The first time, he was nervous, but then he got used to it. Although he enjoys the visits, he wouldn't want to move back permanently. He still doesn't like the Communists, alleging that the entire society runs on bribes, "so much that they don't count the bribe money, they weigh it!"

America's war in Vietnam created refugees, most of whom ended up in the United States, although considerable numbers also went to Canada, Australia, and France. Before the war, most Vietnamese didn't travel or move very far, but now Vietnamese people live all over the world. Pho, a spicy beef and rice noodle soup, is eaten on every continent. Boiseans, like most Americans, also eat cha gio (crispy fried rolls with lettuce and dipping sauce), and banh mi (sandwiches with Vietnamese sausage and pickles on a French roll).

The list of international influences, in both directions, goes on. Vietnam and the United States have a trade agreement, and Vietnamese products (flower pots and clothing are the most noticeable items) show up in American stores. Vietnamese Americans, like most immigrant groups, send remittance money back to family members still in Vietnam. Vietnamese with American relatives try to arrange paperwork in order to legally immigrate to the United States. Boise State University professor Nancy Napier has arranged a student exchange program with a business school in Hanoi.

The Vietnamese refugees who arrived in Boise between 1975 and 1997 set a precedent for future relationships between Idaho and other groups of refugees. As time went on, the state received refugees from other countries: Laotians, Cambodians, Poles, Czechs, Cubans, and Russian Pentecostals arrived in Idaho in the 1980s and 1990s. At the national level, receiving refugees was one U.S. strategy to combat Communism. At the local level, Boiseans began by taking in the first group of people that arrived literally on the doorstep of the Adult Learning Center at Boise State. They continued to take in whoever came, and the emphasis was never much on what ideology people represented but more on the concrete process of helping someone in need. The community got good at working out the details: teaching practical English, giving driving lessons, conducting supermarket tours, helping to fill out job applications, making people feel welcome. From the beginning, Idaho's effort was ad hoc, improvised, informal, and bottom-up not top-down. Above all, it was practical and friendly.

Pho (noodle soup), cha gio (crunchy rolls), and banh mi (baguette sandwiches) are Vietnamese favorites in Boise.

KATHLEEN RUBINOW HODGES holds a master's in history from Boise State University. An author and historian, she is the former director of Idaho's oral history program.

3 | Chosen to Survive

A Bosnian, cut down by shrapnel, sees his life as a miracle.

By Refik Sadikovic with Kathleen Rubinow Hodges

Refik Sadikovic, lanky and tall, is a clear head higher than most other people. A refugee from the Bosnian War, he wants Boiseans to know what it was like. Last fall, Refik talked to editor Kathleen Rubinow Hodges at Boise State University, where he teaches and pursues a doctorate in education. A refugee, he explained, is different from an immigrant who searches for jobs and a better life: "Refugees left their country because of war, and fear, and persecution. They are desperate enough to risk their lives, to cross dangerous borders and seas. They just want to have a peaceful life. They don't have any choice."

Describe your life in Bosnia before the war began. Where did you grow up?

I was raised on a farm in northwest Bosnia, one of the six constituent republics in former Yugoslavia. We had a family of eleven: four brothers, three sisters, my grandma, my parents, and me. When we weren't in school, we worked on our farm. We had a lot of land. We planted orchards and made everything organic. I had a nice childhood, going to school, enjoying peace and freedom.

The small town of Vrnograč, where I went to elementary school, is located fourteen kilometers from the municipality of Velika Kladuša, where I rode the bus each day for an hour to attend high school. During the 1970s and 1980s, Velika Kladuša became the corporate headquarters of Agrokomerc, one of the biggest food companies in former Yugoslavia. Agrokomerc made Velika Kladuša one of the most advanced regions in Yugoslavia. The population of Velika Kladuša was around 20,000 people. My town, Vrnograč, consisted of around 5,000 people. In the center of Vrnograč on the hill, there is an old castle built in the 14th century. Around the castle there were houses and a few roads that led to people's homes where everybody knew each other. We lived a peaceful life until 1991 when the wars in Yugoslavia started. Since Velika Kladuša and Vrnograč are located on the border of Croatia, every day we heard grenades hitting homes located a few miles away in Croatia.

Refik Sadikovic with parents, 1978.

Previous page: Sadikovic returns to Vrnograč, 2013.

And how old were you then?

I was 17 years old, and I was a junior in high school. Students in my school were scared, because we never had experienced something like that before. At that time in the former Yugoslavia, all male citizens were subject to military recruitment, and until you served in the military for a year you couldn't get a passport or leave the country. Because I was 16 years old, I couldn't get a passport. When I turned 18 and finished my high school, I had to join the Bosnian army and fight in the war. My two older brothers, who served in the military earlier, were lucky to leave Bosnia before the war.

The war in Croatia started in 1991. The war in Croatia occurred between Serbs and Croats, because the secessionist Serb Republic of Serbian Krajina was proclaimed in 1991 in Croatia. The war in Bosnia started in April 1992, which was fought between Bosniaks, Serbs and Croats. The Yugoslavian People's Army joined the Serb paramilitary forces in Bosnia and Croatia to fight together with Serbs against the Croats and Bosniaks to create a homogeneous "Great Serbia." Our Bosnian northwest region was completely surrounded by Serbian paramilitary forces in Croatia and Bosnia.

Complicated! You ended up in a refugee camp. How did that happen?

Sadikovic in the Bosnian army, 1994.

In 1993, I was required to join the Bosnian army, the Fifth Corps. I had just finished my high school in June, and the same month I was required to attend military training in a town about 20 miles away. The training was in a school building, a thousand soldiers, all about 18 years old. After my 30-day training, I was defending the city of Bosanska Krupa from the Serbian forces. I stayed there for two months. Then I went back to fight for my town, and I stayed there fighting the war for maybe a year. In July of 1994, we couldn't defend our town anymore, and we decided to escape into Croatia to save the civilians. About 30,000 to 40,000 refugees went together, leaving everything behind.

We escaped to a town called Turanj in central Croatia. It was a no man's land where the Serbian and Croatian forces were separated by the United Nations Protection Force (UNPROFOR). There were no standing buildings in the town. The abandoned and damaged houses, overgrown bushes, and tall grass were full of land mines. We tried to demine the entrances to the houses for the refugees to find a shelter from the rain and cold. We put our lives in danger to help thousands of women and children find a place to sleep.

On the bridge over the river Korana that separates Turanj from the city of Karlovac, the Croatian military yelled, "No, we won't let any refugees enter the Croatian controlled territory." And the horrors of the war were chasing us. I still remember the river Korana with the Croatian tanks blocking the bridge. The bridge was our only way to freedom. I still remember the cruel voice saying, "Nobody can go." No women, no children, nobody. And all around the river they had military watching. Across the river, people had homes in the city of Karlovac, and if we could have moved there we could have established a livable refugee camp. But we ended up building a camp on the street around the mines. Trying to demine the area, some

A Croatian tank guards the Bosnian border, 1998.

Kuplensko refugee camp, Croatia, 1995.

people lost their legs, some people died. We stayed there from July until November of 1994. UNPROFOR brought water and some bread, but that wasn't nearly enough for so many people to survive.

I was so desperate. One day I said, "Okay, I have to leave the camp," and I swam across the river during the night. I wasn't aware that there were tank mines on the other side, laid by the Croatian military. I was shocked when in the middle of the field, I saw anti-tank mines around me. I paused for a minute, thinking about my family and my life in Bosnia. And I

Sign warns of land mines near Vrnograč, Bosnia, 2013.

said, "If I go back, so many mines are behind me as well. So, I will not go back. If I die, you know, I will die and that's it. There is no going back." After I crossed the field safely, I was happy to be alive. I remember it was late fall, cold and foggy weather. Croatians were fighting in that area earlier, and I saw trenches in the ground from previous fights. I mostly walked during the night through the forests, avoiding occupied areas. On my way to Slovenia, I crossed two more rivers. The second river, Kupa, is on the border between Slovenia and Croatia. After roughly five days of walking I came to Slovenia.

Late at night, I came to my eldest sister's apartment. I took a shower and I went to bed. About two hours later, I heard a loud banging at the door and men yelling, "Police, open the door!" in Slovenian. The police said to my sister, "He, the refugee, has to go back." I don't know how they knew I was there. My frightened sister asked, "Why? I will support him. He did nothing wrong. He just escaped the war." I told my sister that everything is going to be okay. I will go with them. They took me back to the river where I crossed the border between

Croatia and Slovenia. They told me, "You crossed the border illegally, and we want to know where you crossed the river." At about 4 a.m., in the middle of the forest, they stopped the car. They said, "We're going to kill you now, and nobody will ever know that you existed," placing a gun on my head. I told them, "If you really want to kill me, do it." Another policeman said, "Okay, let's first go to see where he crossed the river before we kill him." The police continued driving. An hour later, I showed them the shallow part of the river where I walked across into Slovenia.

The Kupa River borders Croatia and Slovenia.

Miraculously they changed their mind, throwing me in front of a judge in his office. After he briefly questioned me, the judge asked me to pay a $200 fine in Slovenian money or spend 30 days in jail. I told him, "I don't have any money to pay you, but I have a request to get a year in jail. Because look, if you send me back to the refugee camp, I might die there. If I get prison for a year I might survive." The judge was livid, and then he ordered the police officers, "Hand him over to the Croatian border patrol!" The truth is, I was happy to go back to camp, because I was afraid they would kill me in Slovenia. At the border the Croatian officers were very nice. They even asked me, "If you want to go back to Slovenia, we will let you go." I said, "No, I don't want to go back to Slovenia, because I am afraid for my life. I would rather go back to the camp."

An hour later, I was back in the camp. Because people were desperate, they decided to start mobilizing to go back and fight for our towns in Bosnia. I was very upset because my dream of being free was destroyed by the Slovenian government: That approach, to return refugees to a place where they faced imminent danger, was against the Geneva Convention. I thought, "Now I will go back and fight for my town, because it's the only place I have." Then people in our camp mobilized 3,000 or 4,000 people who were fit for the military, and we went back to Bosnia. The civilians, mostly women, children, and elderly people, stayed in the camp. They came back to Bosnia two months after we were able to liberate our towns. And we stayed there until July of 1995 when we lost the fight and were forced to flee again.

Headstones mark the 1991 attack on Bosnia's Srebrenica. More than 7,000 Bosniaks died.

That was when you were wounded?

It was July 10, 1995. I could see my house from the hill where I was wounded. I was talking to my comrade about the life after the war, and then I heard a big blast. I remember I only saw something like a long tunnel and a bright light far away. "Am I dead? That is it, I am dying. But it is too early for me to go." I started thinking about my family and friends. And my father had died just a few months earlier. I thought, "My father died. Now I am going to die. How is my family going to handle this?" I was thinking about everything my people and I went through. My life during the war was like living on the edge of dying every day because I suffered so much, fighting every day, being cold, wet, and hungry.

After a few minutes, which seemed to me like eternity, I started seeing figures of people around me. "I actually may not be dead!" I thought. "I might die, but for now I am alive." My comrades were patching my wounds. I had about 15 wounds on my body. I could hear people and I was conscious! My wounds were horrifying, like my shoulder, I could see bones. My hands, arm, chest, mouth were bleeding. My friends had to carry me in a blanket through the forest to an emergency vehicle. And I was thinking I was going to die before I got to the hospital in my town. It took the paramedics half an hour to get me to a hospital.

The hospital had never performed any surgical procedures before the war, because it was only for primary care. The doctor and nurses were moving me from one table to another as they tried to clean and patch my wounds and take X-rays to locate various pieces of shrapnel. As there was no anesthesia, I could feel pain and see the doctor fighting for my life. The doctor was really concerned about the shrapnel in my chest, and he was trying to find it. The look on his face revealed that he could not. I was concerned, but I thought that the shrapnel is in my muscle and it's fine if it stays there. After a two-hour-long procedure, the doctor sent me to a room for critically wounded people. The next morning, the doctor came to see me. When he entered the room, I was sitting. I couldn't use my hands, but I could walk. I was able to go to the restroom by

M-75 Yugoslav hand grenade, 1995

The author inspects a fragment of shrapnel that migrated from his chest to his leg over the course of 16 years.

myself, and he said to the nurses, "Now I know he is going to survive, and he can be moved to a recovery room." I was very happy when I heard that. I thought, "It is not my turn to die. I got another chance."

You have a story about the shrapnel.

Since I was wounded, I had shrapnel in my chest. I never knew it was in the artery. I have so much shrapnel still in my body, and they don't bother me. In 2011, I had a CAT scan after a car accident. After the scan, my doctor told me, "Everything is fine, except you have a piece of metal in your upper leg. And that's probably from the war, because you were wounded." I said, "But I was never wounded in my leg!"

I was somewhat scared. My doctor referred me to a general surgeon. After the surgeon examined me, he said, "Refik, you were never wounded in the leg. Shrapnel can't move through the tissue but through your vein or arteries. I think you were wounded in the chest by the heart, and somehow shrapnel entered your artery and traveled down." And he said, "I have to refer you to a cardiovascular surgeon."

The cardiovascular surgeon, Dr. Gilbertson, did an ultrasound. He stated, "The shrapnel is in your artery and blocking the flow of your blood. If you want, you can have the surgery tomorrow morning, at 9 o'clock." To calm me down, he added, "The shrapnel in the artery, it is something new for me but do not worry."

After the surgery, the doctor gave me the shrapnel in a vial as a gift. He told me, "That shrapnel stayed there at the same place for 16 years. A miracle stopped the shrapnel there, and then your body created tissue around it so it couldn't move." He said, "Your body really protected you, because it surrounded your shrapnel very well with the tissue and expanded the artery to allow the normal blood flow."

Belma and Refik Sadikovic, TEDx Boise, 2016.

You told this story as part of a TED talk. Why did you decide to share it?

I had the surgery in 2011, and finally I shared the shrapnel story at a TED talk in April 2016. I never wanted to show that to anybody because it was kind of a piece of me, and I wasn't ready to share it. I almost felt as if there was still a piece of me in that vial. I didn't like talking about my experience in the war, because whenever I wanted to talk about it I started thinking, "Why did it happen to me? How did I survive?" After the surgery, I asked the doctor, "Can you please explain to me how the shrapnel came to my leg?" The doctor said, "I really can't give you a good explanation. There are only two options. One option, if you were wounded in the artery, you would bleed to death in a matter of minutes. The miracle is that the shrapnel stopped in the artery and didn't pass through. Or the second option is that you were wounded in the heart but then you would be dead as well. That's why I can't explain it to you."

And since then, I tried not to think about it. But my shrapnel reminded me of the purpose of life. I believe that if you do good things in life, you will be protected. Because during the war I was helping people: I didn't want to kill anybody, because I felt like if you kill anybody, even if that person is your enemy, it will come back somehow to bite you. Somehow, I was chosen to survive and I am here to share my story. My body was full of shrapnel, 15 wounds, and miraculously I survived.

I always think about that shrapnel, and so many foreign bodies that are inside, and at peace with me. And people ask if I feel anything. No, I don't! I never felt anything, and even though some of the shrapnel pieces broke my bones, they don't bother me.

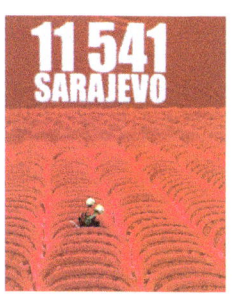

Empty red chairs memorialize the 11,541 victims of the Siege of Sarajevo, Bosnia, 1992-1996.

Quite a story! Now, going back to 1995, did it take long to recover from your wounds?

I remember the day I was wounded. By August, our military was losing ground again. I stayed in the hospital for 10 or 11 days. Then for a second time, about 30,000 civilians were forced to flee to Croatia. There was chaos, panic. People were scared, running. There was a big truck standing outside of the hospital to transport wounded people. I got outside and I tried to get into the truck but I couldn't, because my wounds were still fresh. Somebody helped me to get in the truck. The grenades were falling around us; people were dying. I witnessed horrible scenes. Thousands of refugees were leaving their homes, their town, escaping without anything. The hospital staff loaded the truck with wounded people, and

National and Ethnic Boundaries in the Balkans, 2014

we escaped the town. Very soon we were in Croatia, feeling safer. So many people now refugees on the road, escaping the war for a second time. I was thinking about life in Bosnia and about the future. I couldn't stop thinking. I said, "This time, it's even worse because I was wounded." This time also, we were stopped 15 miles from the Bosnian border by the Croatian military and their tanks. The Croatian soldiers said again, "Nobody can move."

The houses there were destroyed, because Serbs and Croats had been fighting in that area since 1991. We had no food, no water, no place to sleep. People were hungry; they were sharing their last pieces of bread. Many were dying of wounds, because medical help wasn't available. You have more than 30,000 people; how are you going to feed everybody? And again, it took more than a week for the UN to bring some food and water.

I was looking to find help to treat my wounds. During the middle of August it was very hot, and it looked very likely that my wounds would become infected if I left them untreated. I

Ruins of Bužim Castle, Bosnia, near the author's hometown.

said, "Man, I'm going to die this time." I saw a UN Red Cross vehicle by the Croatian checkpoint. After I asked for help, they weren't very friendly. But one of the doctors was really nice. He treated my wounds and gave me some antibiotics. He told me to come again in two days. After a few visits, I was surprised when I saw my deep wounds healing pretty fast. At this camp I stayed with my mother, two brothers, and a sister, as they escaped the war as well. After several days, I started feeling better. Now, again I could shave my face with my hands. I started thinking about leaving the camp again.

Tell me about your second escape.

Two weeks later, my mother said, "You should go and save your life. What if they force you to go back again and fight? Better go and save your life." This time, I decided not to stay in Slovenia but to go straight to Austria. I walked again for six days. I had some food with me. I carried some chlorine tablets that I received from the UN personnel at the camp for the disinfection of water. After I crossed into Austria, I purchased a train ticket and I rode the train to Vienna.

Bombed-out Sarajevo, Bosnia, 1992.

I knew that there was an asylum center in a small town called Traiskirchen. I was told if you reach it, you will be protected from deportation. I was lucky enough to reach that asylum center. At the gate of the asylum, I handed them my ID. It was expired, the picture was damaged, and you could barely see or read anything. I said in the German language, "I am this person. I am a refugee from Bosnia. If you can, please help me." The people were friendly. In a few minutes, they handed me a temporary ID, and they said, "Refik, you are now protected." For several days, I couldn't believe that I was free, again free. I thought I was dreaming. That was one of the very happiest days of my life, but still, I was waking up in the middle of the night thinking I was on the first line of defense and somebody was attacking us.

After a few days, I was resettled to Linz, Austria. Linz was a very nice and welcoming city. I got a place to stay and I received food vouchers for a cafeteria, but we were not allowed to work. Amnesty International helped me file an application for asylum. However, two years later, in 1998, I received a letter that my asylum claim was denied, and I had to leave again.

I left Austria and I went to the American embassy in Zagreb, the capital of Croatia, where I filed an application to be resettled to the United States as a refugee. I explained that I was a soldier in Bosnia, that I was wounded, that I applied for asylum in Austria, and that my application was denied, and I am afraid to go to back to Bosnia. Finally, in December of 1999, I was approved to be resettled in America. I had to go through a cultural orientation class to learn about American life before my flight.

My flight was scheduled for February 26, 2000. I was so happy, finally to be able to leave, and be protected, and get a permanent place to start life. In Austria, I stayed for two years but I wasn't allowed to work. I thought, in America I would finally be able to work! At Zagreb airport, resettlement officials said, "Sign this paper that you are going to repay the airplane ticket, or you can't go." People sometimes think that taxpayers pay everything for refugees, but even an airplane ticket you don't get for free. I had no money or anything, but after resettlement I was $700 in debt. When I landed in Chicago, I received an I-94 visa. I was free again! Since the age of 16, I was in war and in constant fear. Finally, I was allowed to start a brand-new life.

Why did you come to Boise?

I came to Boise because I had a sister living here who was my sponsor. For five weeks, I attended English classes at a Refugee Center over on Jefferson Street, and then I was offered a job. I was told in order to get federal benefits you have to accept the first job offer. I was eager to learn English, but I had to accept the job, which was with Pavement Specialties of Idaho (PSI). I operated a street sweeper, and I worked about 30 to 40 hours overtime every week for almost three years. Even though I couldn't speak English very well, I was very good at my job. I became a supervisor, because there were many Bosnian refugees hired at that time, because that was kind of a hard job and not many people wanted to do it. Besides working as a street sweeper operator, I was creating work schedules for other sweeper operators' routes. I loved my first job. I was making very good money, because of overtime, which paid time and a half. I could afford things that I never thought I would be able to afford.

USA/Bosnia and Herzegovina flag pin

Later you went to work for Micron. How did that happen?

We were sweeping Micron streets on the weekends. Sometimes I would be over there working all night, and thinking, "I like technology and these are really good jobs. So, I should apply." In April 2004, I gained enough courage to apply for a job at Micron, and I was hired. But I kept my job at PSI for about two more months to train new people.

My PSI boss, Keith Lewis, was very encouraging. He said, "If you want to stay and need a raise, I will give you a raise. But if you want to leave, I respect that. And if you ever want to come to work for me just let me know, and I will have a job for you." I've met with Keith several times since then, and we are always happy to talk about experiences we had.

Graduation, Boise State University, 2015.

At Micron at the beginning, I was an operator making much less than I was making at PSI. But because of my strong technology background on various applications and computer hardware and software skills, I advanced quickly. I sometimes fixed equipment and helped technicians and engineers troubleshoot. My manager and supervisor told me, "We have Boise State University and College of Southern Idaho classes offered at the Micron site. After you start taking the required classes, we will be able to give you a manufacturing technician job." I took some classes and I was promoted. First, I was a manufacturing technician, and then after I graduated I got an engineering technician job.

But in 2009, microchips started losing value, and Micron laid off workers. The management at Micron offered to relocate me to their Lehi, Utah, Micron plant or the Manassas plant near Washington, D.C. I said, "No, I don't want to leave Boise. I would like to continue my education." And they told me, "If you don't want to go, you will get a severance package, and then you can go to school." In 2010, I got my degree in criminal justice, and then I got my Bachelor of Applied Science. In 2013, I started my master's degree in education. I graduated in 2015, and I applied to the doctorate program to pursue my doctorate in education, curriculum and instruction. I am planning to start my dissertation in the summer of 2017.

Tell me more about your decision to go back to school.

I strongly believe that encouragement is very important. When I was at Micron, I was told, "You should start taking classes." I thought that people were joking with me. "I am not good enough. My English is not very good, and I don't think I will be able to do that." They said, "Look, you know how to fix equipment that you never saw in your life. We are sure you will be fine." I was encouraged to pursue college. Finally, I was able to fulfill my dream to continue my education that was disrupted by the bombs years ago in Bosnia. Many people supported that dream and they believed in me, and I didn't want to disappoint them.

This is why whenever I talk with refugee students in high schools, I encourage them. I say "Look, I came to America and I didn't go to an American high school. I was able to finish college and now I'm getting my doctorate. I had to work much harder, because writing was much harder for me than for somebody who attended an American high school."

Bosnian dancer, World Refugee Day, Boise.

The only English I knew was from TV, and from listening to the NPR radio in my truck during my work. As somebody who is from a different country, I felt like if I didn't know something, people will judge me and laugh at me. If an American doesn't know how to spell, that's fine; but if a foreigner doesn't know how to spell, it's embarrassing. I felt that I had to prove my worthiness to others. But you should believe in yourself and not give up. Don't let fear or insecurity or anything or anyone else discourage you. That is my advice.

I wanted to ask some more questions about yourself and other Bosnians here. What surprised you the most when you got to the United States?

In America, many things were similar to my country. For instance, I had a driver's license before I came here. It was easy for me to get an Idaho driver's license, because the traffic rules are similar to the traffic rules in Europe. The only thing that was hard for me was the language barrier. At the beginning, I would go to the store to buy something, and I would spend more time trying to find items because I didn't know how to ask for help. I felt that I was educated and well-rounded, but just because of the one thing, speaking the English language, at times I felt desperate.

Celebrating Bosnian Heritage Day, Boise, 2015.

Are Bosnians in Boise a community?

The Bosnians are a community here. In Boise, we have about 3,500 to 4,000 people. We have a few Bosnian stores: Bo-Ex on Emerald and Orchard, Europe Delicious on Fairview and Mitchell, and the Sofra Grill on Overland Road in Meridian. We also have singers coming every couple of months, and people gather for those events and dance Bosnian folk dances. We meet at Europe Delicious for coffee, to socialize, and speak Bosnian. Also, we have an annual Bosnian Heritage Day each year in May. The event lasts all day. People celebrate the Bosnian culture with food, music, dance, and sport. The Bosnian community is pretty small; people know each other and stay together. Most Bosnians that came as refugees 17 or 18 years ago own their businesses and their houses. Many of them own construction businesses. If you want to build your house, you almost can do anything with a Bosnian company, because Bosnians are really well known for very good construction work over there in Europe.

Are there people here from other parts of former Yugoslavia?

Right now, here in Boise, we have Bosnians, and we have Serbians and Croatians. Most Serbians here are of Serbian nationality, but they are from Croatia, because during the Serbian-Croatian war they were expelled from Croatia. In Boise, Bosnians are the biggest group, and we have a smaller Serbian and Croatian community here.

Spinach pie zeljanica, a Bosnian favorite.

Have you gone back to Bosnia to visit?

Yes, I've visited Bosnia about seven or eight times since I resettled to the U.S. Our family house is empty now. I have four brothers and two sisters over there in Europe, but nobody is in Bosnia. We have some neighbors that take care of the house when we are away. Now it's peaceful there. And I think if the situation was like now, I would have never left in the first place. But people always ask, would you like to go back? When I visit, I always look at my ticket and say, "Oh, in seven or eight days I am going back home," because I have been living in Boise almost 17 years and I feel this is my home now.

Socializing over Bosnian coffee is an hours-long ritual.

Tell me something about the classes you teach.

I am in the Ed.D. program in curriculum and instruction. I teach University Foundation courses and a couple of workshops. One is Refugees, Languages, and Cultures in Idaho; and the other workshop is Bosnians, From Refugee Camps to American Citizenship. In that class, we talk about Bosnian culture, history, and the Bosnian War. I also teach a language course, Bosnian 101.

I started teaching Bosnian 101, because Bosnian youth are losing their language and culture. In 2011, I met a Bosnian girl in one of my classes. Other students told me, "She's Bosnian." I started speaking in Bosnian to her. And she replied, "No, I don't speak Bosnian." She said, "I'm ashamed to speak Bosnian. I do not want my friends to hear me." And then her friends

Neighbors United helps refugees resettle in Boise.

asked, "Say something, please, say something in Bosnian." "No, no, I don't want to say anything in Bosnian." It felt really awkward that Bosnians are ashamed to speak their own language. That means they're ashamed of their parents as well, and their heritage. Because if you're ashamed to speak Bosnian, that means if anybody sees you with your parents, you will be ashamed because they speak Bosnian, right? So I decided to create a Bosnian language class to encourage Bosnian youth to learn and to preserve their language. I have heard from Bosnian students in Boise saying, "Man, we have a Bosnian class at Boise State! It's so cool." One Bosnian, after he took the Bosnian class, said, "Oh, now, after taking this class I want to go and visit Bosnia. It is such a beautiful country." The Bosnian course had a positive effect on him. Therefore, the Bosnian classes, the workshops, and Bosnian Heritage Day should be used to help young kids get acculturated in both cultures, to make sure that they don't see their parents, language, or culture as an embarrassment.

Are you also involved in city or university organizations?

Yes, I'm co-founder of two student groups: the Boise State Refugee Alliance and the Bosnian Student Association. I'm also a member of the Boise City Neighbors United steering committee and a member of the Refugee Social Integration staff committee. Also at Boise State, I'm a member of the Cultural and Ethnic Diversity board and a member of the Boise State Community Refugee Collaboration team. We meet every few months, and we talk about refugee issues and resettlement in Boise. All together we can make a difference, and we can help people that are struggling, and dying, and who want to have a good life.

When we help refugees, they benefit our community because they pay taxes, you know: property taxes, state taxes, federal taxes. When I came, after a few weeks, I started working and paying taxes. And I wasn't really against that. Look, I am making enough money; I should be helping other people, because nothing is free. Refugees really help the community because they are willing to work, and usually, refugees are mostly younger, working age.

What do you miss about Bosnia?

I miss friends and family. I miss time, the simplicity of life over there, the ability to slow down. And going out for coffee with friends in Bosnia, which is like having social time that lasts for hours. If you visit a coffee shop in Bosnia, you will see people talking about politics, the government, gossiping, and all that. And also I miss wild nature, like the nature of my village.

When you tell your story to other Idahoans, what do you hope they will learn?

Any refugee, Bosnians or any others, they left their country because of war and because of fear and persecution. And they just want a life without fear, a life without war, where they can be productive and free. Most of them just want to be happy and to have a peaceful life, because they suffered so

Clubs and an undergraduate minor support refugee studies at Boise State.

Near the author's house where he was wounded in 1995.

much. They did not leave their home country because they just wanted to go on vacation. Think about yourself leaving your place empty-handed and going thousands of miles away. Would you do that if nobody's forcing you? Refugees just want to work and they are ready to start new lives. When I see refugees fleeing now in boats, crossing borders in Bulgaria or Greece, I see myself, because what's happening to them now looks exactly like what happened to me 20 years ago.

I hope that through my story, people will learn more about refugee struggles around the world. Refugees are victims of world instability that wasn't created by the refugees. However, many people still blame refugees for coming to their countries, as if refugees are the cause of everything that is going on in our world. I was desperate to risk my life to get to Austria, and I can tell you that all refugees are desperate enough to cross dangerous borders and seas. Refugees are not different from me - from us. How would you feel if you were forced to flee your country and you had to walk hundreds of miles without anything, only to find that some western countries (like Slovenia in my case) do not want you, and in fact they hate you, they deport you, just because you are a refugee?

Currently, I am Bosnian American. I succeeded in my life, and I am happy. But should I stop caring about other people in the world who are still experiencing things similar to what

Standing in the spot of the near-fatal shrapnel explosion, 2013.

I experienced? I can't! I can't stop caring. I can't let them suffer more, because I am not a person who thinks, "Better to seek happiness in your own life than worry about others born under some unlucky stars." Based on my life and my teaching, I strongly believe we should treat every human being with the dignity and respect that we expect to receive. I have shared my refugee story with students, coworkers, friends, and many good people in our community. Many of them were very supportive toward me and other refugees. Thus I hope that my story will change how people see the refugees that are fleeing to save their lives. With just a little support and resources, refugees grow and give back. It is time we as a nation begin to see refugees not merely as liabilities but as assets. Not as burdens but as becoming. And isn't that what this country is about?

REFIK SADIKOVIC is completing a doctorate in education at Boise State University, where he teaches language, ethics, and multiculturalism.

Verse: *Living Witness*

By Fidel Mwendambali Nshombo

You were there when they were killing them
You were there when they disappeared,
It was not an easy thing to bear,
I understand it hurts,
I know it's painful
And I know this not because I heard,
But I was there with you
We shared the same pain.
We went through the same torture,
We suffered the same loss
But it's time to change and move on
Because we are a living witness

I understand you hate them,
You always talk about revenge,
But that's not what I am about,
I had moved on so long now,
And so you should because,
Not every Hutu is my brother
not every Tutsi is my enemy
Not every Congolese my friend,
Not every Rwandese my enemy
I am a man of peace,
And peace is my friend and my brother
I will spread peace around the world
I will take no part in your revenge
I will take no part in your evil deeds
And I will never do the evil you want to do,
I have seen what you've seen,
I've suffered what you suffered
I've endured the pain that you endured
But I don't know what you know
And I don't want to do what you do
And I certainly don't believe in revenge that You believe in
I believe in God, love, peace and forgiveness
I have moved on so long now, and so you should

I'm a living witness, now I know that...
And so you should be.

From *Route to Peace: The Cries of the Forgotten Refugees in Deadly Camps* (2009).

FIDEL MWENDAMBALI NSHOMBO is a Boise-based poet from the Democratic Republic of Congo.

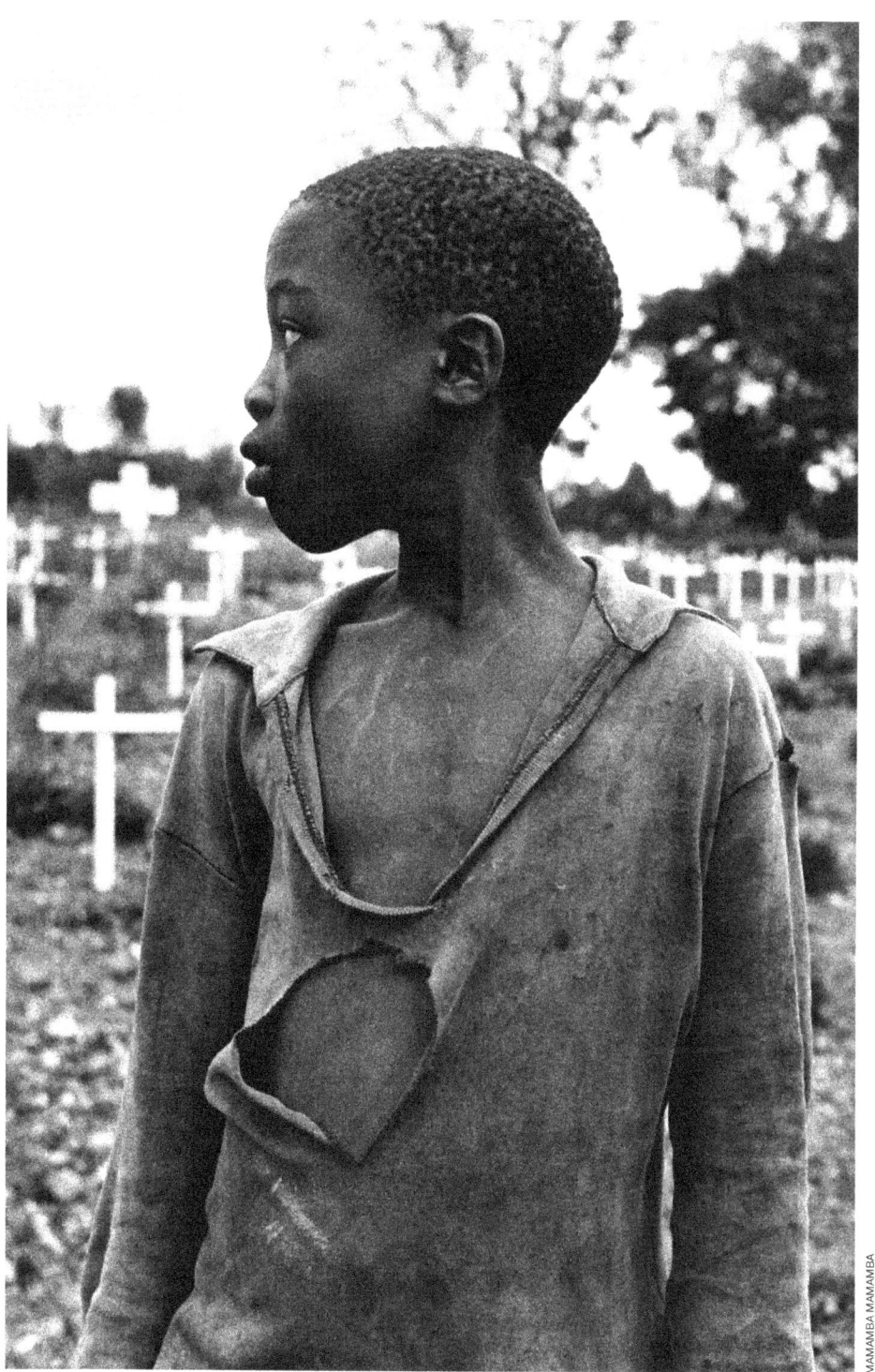

A living witness stands in a graveyard, Rwanda, 2013.

4 Leave One to Remember

A child's name bears witness to his mother's Rwandan struggle.

By Laura Winslow

Emelda Nzobhampari came to Boise after years in Tanzanian camps. She is now an employee in a job readiness program administered by Sarah Priddy. In the fall of 2016, Sarah helped Emelda tell her story to author Laura Winslow.

Emelda, age 27, still carries memories from the horrors of Rwanda, horrors which few from her village survived. "What did I do to be here instead of all the others?" she wonders. "What did I have to offer?"

Slender and dark with a glowing smile, Emelda dabs tears with a crumple of Kleenex. She was five in 1994 when she last saw her parents. Her father had been a businessman; her mother, a teacher. Inquisitive as a child, she dreamed of going to school and having her chance to learn. She recalls her mother's promise: whether schooled or not, she would prosper. "It is not school that makes you successful," says Emelda quoting her mother. "It is your knowledge and your willingness to learn. If you are kind and smile, and you tell people that they are special to you, you will be successful in life."

It's a scorching Boise day as Emelda tells her story, and the office is a cool retreat from the weather. Emelda was a student at Full Circle Exchange and now works as a chocolatier in one of the organization's adjacent buildings. "We provide a pathway to empowerment," Sarah explains, "so it's really about each woman, individually." Full Circle Exchange's U.S. Job Readiness Training Program (JRTP) offers refugee women in Boise, as well as women who are transitioning out of poverty, the stepping stones to self-sufficiency. Sarah is director of the Boise JRTP and is also one of the teachers for the classes the women take. Over time, Sarah has become a friend and advocate to these women as well.

Rwandan Refugee Crisis

Kagera River winds along the entire border between Tanzania and Rwanda. The only land crossing between the two nations is a two-lane cement bridge with yellow railings. The Rusomo bridge extends over the rapids and waterfall of the same name.

In April 1994 more than 200,000 people crossed the Rusumo Bridge into Tanzania.

Previous page: Emelda Nzobhampari, 2017.

Looking across the bridge into Rwanda, there are hills covered in elephant grass. The valleys between the hills and the bridge itself are cradled by thick rain forest.

Everything is green except the river, which is red and opaque. In 1994, the Rusomo bridge, the rain forest in the valleys, and the hills reaching for the skies were covered in a terrifying tidal wave of people. In May of that year, the *New York Times* explained that the slow throng of Rwandan refugees walking into Tanzania was over 10 miles long. Funneled onto the narrow bridge, they crossed the border: 10,000 people per hour.

People were carrying anything they could, from mattresses to radios, from cooking ware to gasoline jugs filled with water. On foot, in wheelbarrows and wheelchairs, balancing a whole group on a single bike, they moved toward the border. Among the people were cows and goats, joining in one of the largest human exoduses of modern times.

People camped around the border post. During the day, the air was filled with animal sounds, people talking, and radio tunes. At night, the air was unbreathable, thick with smoke rising from the campfires in the grass. Along the border entry,

Rwandans crowd into a makeshift border encampment, 1994.

piles of machetes and hoes were abandoned in exchange for safety.

Once in the camps, the air wasn't much better. Disease was the main concern, and the bodies of people who had tried to flee from death littered the streets. The *New York Times* wrote about this again in July 1994, describing the smell of rotting animals and humans. Trucks moved bodies to mass graves, unable to keep up with the thousands of deaths per day.

The men and women, and all the children who were born and grew up in Tanzanian refugee camps, remained years without knowing their fate. Some were dragged into the forests and killed in vengeance. Others walked back to Rwanda, hoping to pick up the pieces of their lives, and still more waited to be sent to some foreign place with promise of a better future. Among the last group was the little girl Emelda.

Emelda

Emelda was 5 years old when she last saw her parents. She was dropped off at her grandparents' home for the Easter holidays in 1994, and her parents told her they would come back to get her when school started again. When school did start up, Emelda was still with her grandparents. Her cousin, who was also staying with them, went off to school and never came back either. Not long after, Emelda's grandparents were killed, and she was all alone.

Amid the chaos, she recognized a man in town and decided to follow him. "He used to visit my grandparents' home," Emelda recalls. "I followed him to another village in Rwanda. He told me that no one could help me there, but if I found my father's family, they would be able to help." The man wrote down Emelda's father's name for her and told her to go to Burundi, where her father's tribe was, to ask for help to find her other grandparents. Emelda made it to Burundi and remembers finding a place where the tribes were gathering. She went to the tribal leader to ask for help finding her family. "He said he recognized the name but couldn't tell me where they were. I begged anyone to help me, to find my family." But no one could. Emelda left Burundi alone.

Making it back to Rwanda, Emelda found the man she had once followed in a town near the Tanzanian border. "That man and his wife were like family to me." Emelda clutches Sarah's hand. "I looked to him as a father." Emelda followed the couple across the border, into the Kagera region of Tanzania, to Rukore refugee camp. As Emelda grew into a teenage girl, the relationship she had with the couple began to change. "He started harassing me," she explains, "threatening to take me back to Rwanda." Sarah breaks in and reminds Emelda that she doesn't have to talk about anything she doesn't want to. Emelda shakes her head, "I need to say this." Her expression is unyielding.

"I told him I had no family to go to," she continues. "I didn't know anyone in Rwanda, and I can never go back there. After everything that happened in Rwanda, I'll never go there again." When Emelda was 16, the harassment twisted into threats of murder. The man that Emelda had once thought could be a father to her was roaring at her that he had taken her in and cared for her. Now, as he was leaving to go back to Rwanda, she had to follow him there, or he would kill her before he left.

Tens of thousands of refugee children died in 1994 when cholera hit Tanzania.

"I ran." Breathing deeply, Emelda continues, "I was so scared. I ran to the UN office in the camp and told them what had happened."

The Office of the United Nations High Commissioner for Refugees (UNHCR) welcomed Emelda, relieved that she had found them, and told her that they would take care of her. "They told me, 'We know it hurts.'" The workers begged Emelda not to bottle up everything she felt and all she had been through, but rather tell people, "They said God will help me find my way to a better future. They were right."

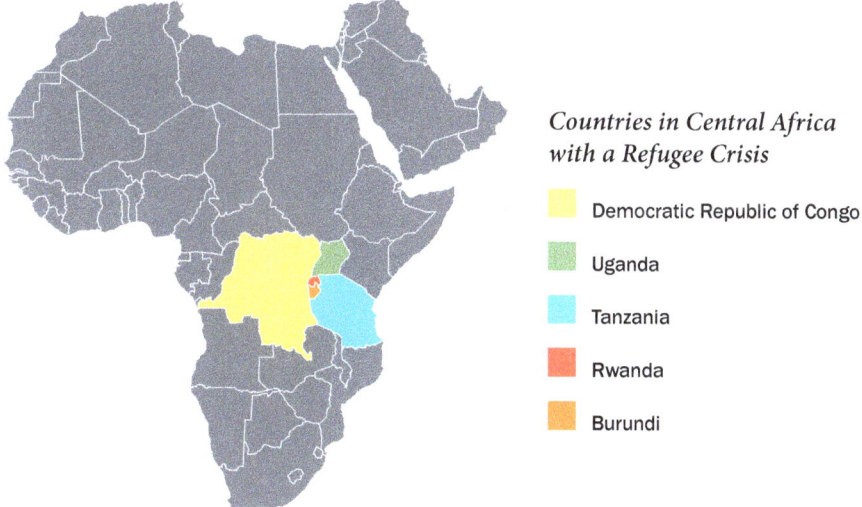

Countries in Central Africa with a Refugee Crisis

- Democratic Republic of Congo
- Uganda
- Tanzania
- Rwanda
- Burundi

Emelda's UNHCR file began in 2005. Her case moved forward quickly, but just as she got the news that she was going to be resettling in Australia, in 2006, Tanzania began pushing some Rwandan refugees back across the border. Rukore camp was on the verge of closing. "We were told to go back to where we came from, that we were no longer welcome there," Emelda relates, turning the withered Kleenex daintily around in her hands. "I was terrified." She said that some were taken from the camp by force; others were told they would be killed if they didn't leave. Emelda knew she couldn't stay there, but she had nowhere else to go. In the nick of time, she was transferred to Mutabira camp.

Full Circle Exchange

Trying to steady her emotions, Emelda explains that everyone she knows – her friends, her family, all of the people she used to see around her – is dead. She is alive. All the officials Emelda encountered were kind, attentive, and understanding, while the other refugees around her were unable to get any bit of help. She breaks off and looks at Sarah. "I love Full Circle Exchange," she says, with striking sincerity. "I have received more than a job here. I have received a family."

Emelda removes the hairnet from her head, exposing perfect braided rows of black hair, with just one bright golden braid catching the light. It's as bright as her eyes when she remembers something important about her past.

Full Circle Exchange is snuggled in among a nest of office buildings on Cole Road in Boise. "Most of the stuff here is donated," says Sarah, pointing out a vintage barn door that decorates one wall of the modest classroom. "The guys that were renovating this room had this lying around and gave it to us." The classroom is part of the Job Readiness Training Program that Sarah runs for Full Circle Exchange.

The program, although still in its early years, has been successful. Local news channel KTVB quotes Sarah stating that JRTP saw a 92 percent job placement rate last year. The missing placement was due to one woman moving away shortly after the end of the program. KTVB describes Full Circle Exchange as a "safe place [for refugee women] to help them move forward with their lives."

A package of Full Circle products assembled by Emelda.

"We take care of the stress first. That is, we give the women an income while they are here so that they don't have to worry about paying rent or the grocery bill. If these women are worried about making ends meet, they won't be open to learning and healing." JRTP offers computer skills training, résumé building skills, English classes, financial literacy, and more, while simultaneously giving the women in the program exposure and training in a wide array of jobs. The program ends with the women receiving a real employment opportunity from a local business right here in Boise.

"For women to successfully rise out of poverty, or adapt to a new place, they first need to feel welcome and wanted." Sarah looks around the classroom at the warm-colored fabrics and small decorations that help to make the place cozy. "We

Sarah Priddy, top left, poses with coworkers at Full Circle Exchange, 2017.

give them that." The program also includes healing through art and music therapy, mentorship, and group counseling. "A lot of the time, women get stuck in a vicious circle of poverty because they can't see the point of getting out. They need to feel important and know that they are worth it. Once you give a woman the sense of empowerment, she can do anything."

Emelda is a JRTP graduate who now works at Happy Day Chocolates, a small chocolate factory that makes ethically-sourced artisan chocolates. "This is how we can give each woman on-the-job training," Sarah explains. "The women work here a few hours a day, have quotas, and experience a real work dynamic with managers, trainers, and co-workers. By having it here and running it ourselves, we can work with the women as they learn the ropes of a typical American business environment."

Custom-made artisan chocolates are crafted by refugees at Happy Day Chocolates in Boise.

Refugees queue to be transferred from Burundi to Nyarugusu camp in Tanzania, 2015.

Remember Emmanuel

Emelda breaks her story and looks up. She lightens up and laughs. "I want to tell you about the boy!" she exclaims. While she was living in the Rukore camp, Emelda met a boy named Emmanuel. She didn't know him well, but they went to the same church and she saw him around. At first, she didn't really care to talk to him, but they had become almost friends when they were both transferred to Mutabira.

"In the Mutabira camp, the UN process involved a series of interviews," Emelda explains. "They want to see who you are and test you to make sure you really are a refugee." Sarah nods, adding that many of the women who have come to Full Circle Exchange have had the same experience. "They ask you these questions about your past. Then, several months later, they ask you again to see if your story matches. It's not a perfect system." The names of people who had passed their interviews would be displayed on the UNHCR office wall.

"Emmanuel and I had to go through the same process," Emelda says, smiling again. "We became closer." They fell in love. "I eventually gave that lucky guy a chance, and we started dating."

Emelda remembers the day an announcer told the camp that there was a new posting of names for all of those who would be resettled to the U.S. "We looked at the names, and mine was there." Emmanuel's name wasn't. The couple was expecting their first child at the time. Emmanuel wanted to add Emelda to his family's file, as he was in the camp with his parents. It would have resulted in everyone being placed back at the beginning of the process without knowing how long they would be stuck in the camp. Emmanuel was to be sent to Canada, and Emelda and the baby were to go to the U.S.

"We wanted to get married," Emelda says, "but we didn't have time. Instead, Emmanuel followed the ways of his father's tribe." Emmanuel hosted a small celebration for his whole family so that they could meet Emelda. His parents accepted her wholeheartedly, and she finally felt safe. "When you are introduced to his family, that is when you know a man truly loves you." She smiles, remembering how she told him: "I love you so much, and I want to grow old with you. I will have your baby, and in the future we will get married and be a family."

Emmanuel's son was born on July 14, 2014. In February of the following year, Emmanuel left for Canada. On their child's first birthday, Emelda walked out of a plane carrying the 1-year-old boy named Remember Emmanuel into Boise, Idaho.

Emmanuel, still in Canada, calls Emelda every day. The two hope to find a way to be together.

LAURA WINSLOW, a native of Denmark, holds bachelor's degrees in sociology and marketing from Boise State University.

5 | Food of the Pharaohs

Tiny teff, grown in Idaho, helps preserve Ethiopian heritage.

By Emily Fritchman

Coffee beans roast on the oven. Spices fill the air. Mother and daughter laugh as they make the traditional Ethiopian flatbread. The spongy bread is called injera. Its tangy sourdough taste comes from a pinch of salt and the fermentation of a tiny golden-brown grain. Teff, the mysterious grain, is a species of African lovegrass. Nutritious and easy to plant, teff, or tef, is transforming high-desert agriculture as the West discovers injera and hungers for gluten-free foods.

Desert sun and irrigation make the volcanic soils of the Boise Valley ideal for transplanting teff. Dry heat likewise appeals to desert descendants from ancient civilizations. Refugees from the Horn of Africa – from Ethiopia, Djibouti, Eritrea, and Somalia – number about 1,300 in Boise-Meridian-Nampa. One is Yordanos Refu, age 27, a refugee from Ethiopia, a teff connoisseur, and our host. Her family fled a war and famine that killed more than a million people. Escaping to a refugee camp in Djibouti and granted U.S. asylum in 2001, the Refu family was sent to Atlanta; but an airport misunderstanding diverted their passage to Boise. Yordanos, the oldest of three siblings, made the most of it with scholarships to Riverstone School and then the College of Idaho. Articulate and determined, she excelled in business and political science. She now works for a Caldwell pioneer who feeds the African diaspora and is one of North America's largest exporters of teff.

"Teff injera to an Ethiopian and Eritrean is what apple pie is to Americans," says Yordanos. "It has been part of my life since birth. It is not far-fetched to say teff is part of my identity."

Yordanos thinks the best place to sample injera is her family's own quiet kitchen near Veterans Memorial Park. Mother Belaynesh pours a gluey batter of teff over a spherical ceramic grill – a mitad. She ladles the batter from the outer edges, swirling inward. She covers the grill while explaining injera's importance. The bread is more than a staple. A cultural ambassador, a food utensil, it is eaten by hand and used like a scoop. How many crepe-like flats does the family cook each day? "As many as my family needs," says Belaynesh, laughing. "I don't count."

MAY SLATER/BOTANICA ETHIOPIA

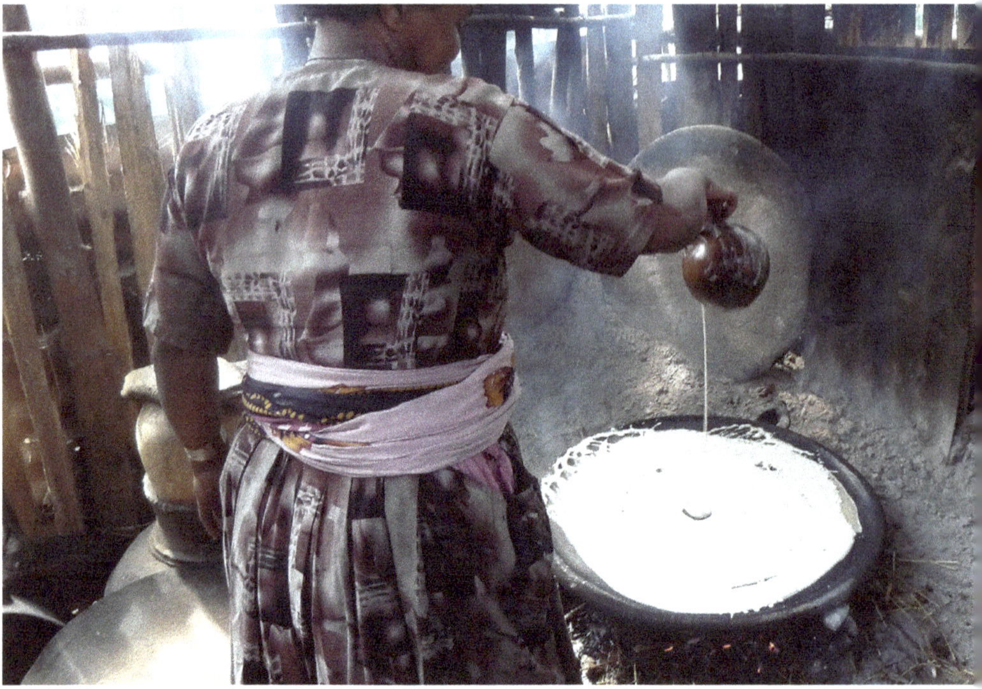

An Ethopian woman makes injera, a crepe-like flatbread made with teff flour. It has a unique, slightly spongy texture with a mild sour and sweet flavor.

Previous page: Wayne Carlson cultivates teff near Boise.

HUFFINGTON POST

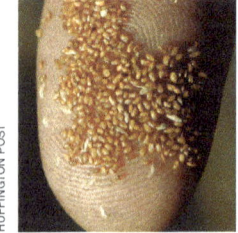

Hundreds of tiny grains of teff can fit on the tip of a finger.

Ancient Nutrition

Ethiopian teff is fast becoming a health-food substitute for spaghetti noodles and other western staples. World consumption, since 2006, has increased more than 50 percent. Mighty but tiny, a single grain of teff measures less than a millimeter. Linguists trace the name to an Amharic word for "lost," which is what happens when grain particles disappear in harvest because of their minuscule size. It takes about 150 seeds of teff to match the weight of a grain of wheat. Yet the world's smallest commercial grain is rich with calcium, iron, protein, potassium, magnesium, and vitamins B6 and C. Its storage proteins are similar to a number of animal products and easy to digest. It is also gluten-free and high in fiber. Easy to plant and filling, it can be used in cereal, stews, soups, and energy bars. Health guru Dr. Mehmet Oz prescribes teff tortillas as a remedy for weight gain and PMS.

Scientists debate whether the African grain is a hybrid species of a seed found in the tombs of pharaohs. Teff, archaeologists say, may have been among the first grains to be cultivated, dating back more than 6,000 years. Pottery shards from the fifth century at Axum resemble the ceramic grills used for baking teff injera. From Ethiopia to India, Australia, and South America, the plant now rivals hay as livestock forage. But only recently has teff made inroads in Europe. Ethiopian authorities litigated in 2007 when a Dutch company patented a hybrid of teff. Patents and trade agreements, they alleged, hiked the price to native consumers. Global prices nearly tripled from 2005 to 2007. But with the grain's celebrity came modern industrial farming methods. Ethiopian teff production has grown by double digits over the last decade.

"[W]ash your hands and get set," advises a Johannesburg publication. "Teff has become a super grain and a favourite. ... Ethiopian food is set for world domination."

Teff Comes to Boise

Wayne Carlson thinks the hot days and cool nights of Snake River agriculture can satiate global demand. A farmer and biologist, he is a 30-year veteran of teff production, and for all that time, he reflects, people have asked him the same incredulous question: Who would want to grow what Africans grow? Carlson calls the question "chauvinistic." Teff, more than a health food, will grow when other crops fail. "Teff is a big part of my diet, just as it is for all Ethiopian athletes." In Ethiopia, "everybody eats injera every day, and they don't get bored."

Carlson's teff adventure began in the 1970s as a Red Cross volunteer during Ethiopia's most murderous drought. He worked in Ethiopia's central highlands where farmers still used oxen to plow. Westerners were determined to increase production with chemical fertilizers. The experience inspired him to experiment with teff back in the States.

In the 1980s Carlson and his wife, Elisabeth, relocated to the Boise Valley. They worked in the seed industry, studied the climate, and purchased a 5-acre farm. "The risks [were] phenomenal," the farmer told a reporter, but then again, he reasoned, "a population of 30 million has been living on [teff] for thousands of years."

A man sifts to separate the grains of teff from the chaff.

One of Carlson's most discriminating customers is a Boise chef who learned to cook in an Ethiopian refugee camp. Kibrom Milash, the son of a shopkeeper, now runs a place of his own in a State Street strip mall. Twinkle lights fall from the ceiling. African tapestries brighten the walls. Twenty-inch flats of injera, served family style without plates or eating utensils, absorb wats (stews) of beef, poultry, lentils, and lamb. Milash, in a polo shirt, greets and dashes about with a beaming smile.

Kibrom Milash feeds Boise's taste for injera in his restaurant west of downtown. Right: rolled flats of teff injera.

Milash, who reached Boise in 2013, worked as a janitor, taxi driver, and coffee-house barista before a business loan financed his dream. He opened a food stall on Franklin Road in the ill-fated Boise International Market. After fire gutted the market, he relocated to State and North 35th. Kibrom's Ethiopian & Eritrean Restaurant quickly became a five-star Yelp sensation with four employees, 40 dishes, and 650 to 700 customers weekly.

"Customers are king," says Milash, who thanks Boise for being so "awesome." Boiseans tip and are eager to help. "I do not feel ashamed to ask for anything," the restaurateur told the *Boise Weekly*. "In America, everything has a solution."

Teff Love

Vegetables and stews scent the Refu family home in northwest Boise. Steam rises from flats of injera served according to the ancient tradition in a colorful basket called a messob. Wooden and ceramic bowls hold spiced greens, chickpeas, and lentils. We tear injera, Ethiopian style, with the right hand only. We finish with coffee roasted over the stove in a long-handled pan. Strong and black and served with a teaspoon of sugar, it brews in an African earthenware pot.

For Ethiopians, Yordanos explains, food is ceremony, a cultural bond. "If you know an Ethiopian, you have eaten teff injera. It is a staple in most every household. In America, I think of teff and injera as doors that lead to questions and discussion, bringing cultures together." Food nurtures the wealth of multicultural understanding. Ethiopian seeds, transplanted to the Boise Valley, cultivate a dynamic that benefits both.

American-grown maskal teff is ground fresh daily by The Teff Company and packaged for retail sale.

EMILY FRITCHMAN is a Boise native and contributor to *The Other Idahoans: Forgotten Stories of the Boise Valley* (2015). A college junior, she is completing a Boise State double major in history and English. Todd Shallat contributed to this chapter.

Gallery: *World Refugee Day*

By Todd Shallat

Londoners bring white umbrellas to the annual celebration. Somalis sing a chorus of thanks to the president of Djibouti. Malaysians download an app for a virtual tour of a tent encampment. Flood lights turn UN cyan blue at the Leaning Tower of Pisa. South Africans release orange balloons.

World Refugee Day, internationally celebrated, commemorates the 1951 Convention Relating to the Status of Refugees – a landmark multinational treaty, the first to acknowledge asylum as a fundamental human right. Its connection to Boise dates back to the cowboy politician who served Idaho in the U.S. Senate at the close of the Second World War. Senator Glen Taylor was an avid proponent of a world federation and asylum for the dispossessed. A half century later, in 2001, the UN designated June 20 as an annual day of awareness. Festivities in Boise began with Bosnian dancing at the Basque Museum.

"World Refugee Day has become a Boise tradition," said Kara Fink of the Idaho Office for Refugees, a festival organizer. "It's through celebrations like this that fear is countered and a more welcoming community is formed."

In 2016 the day began with accordion music and the thumping bass of West African drums. Boys and girls in sashes and scarves linked arms as they jangled and jumped through the choreographed steps of a Bosnian folk dance. The scent of garlic and cilantro rose from kabobs and pastries. A vendor sold African fabrics. In City Hall Plaza, meanwhile, 17 new Americans swore oaths of allegiance, having waited five years and passed their naturalization exams. All refugees resettled in Boise, they were Bhutanese, Bosnian, Burmese, Iranian, Iraqi, Somali-Bantu, Ukrainian, and Vietnamese. Everyone, for the moment, seemed grateful. New citizens clutched tiny American flags.

"I wouldn't miss it for the world," said Fidel Nshombo, a Congolese refugee. At age 12, separated from family, he began an 11-year trek through seven African countries, reaching Idaho in 2006. That June 20 was his first refugee day in Boise. Two years later, an accomplished poet, he was master of ceremonies.

"I honestly thought at the time that I was the only refugee here," said Nshombo, recalling his first years in Boise. "Refuge day wasn't then what it is now."

World Refugee Day is now like a family reunion, tearful and joyous, an extravaganza of colors and sounds. On tap for 2017 are Burmese dancers, Burmese dumplings, Somali sambusas, jewelry, textiles, and hand-stitched Ethiopian dolls. New Americans will again crowd into City Hall Plaza for a collective oath of allegiance. Soccer teams will compete for the second annual Refugee Day tournament trophy, before Boiseans sitting under pastel umbrellas in Ann Morrison Park.

"Refugees would like to have the same problems you have." World Refugee Day promotion, Buenos Aires, 2010.

Karen dancers, The Grove Plaza, Boise, June 20, 2015.

Irish World Refugee Week, Dublin, 2016.

Commemorative postage stamp for the 1951 Convention Relating to the Status of Refugees, Tajikistan, 2001.

Boise-made African sandals, The Grove Plaza, Boise, June 23, 2012.

Rwandan baskets, The Grove Plaza, Boise, June 23, 2012.

Citizenship ceremony, The Grove Plaza, Boise, June 23, 2012.

Citizenship ceremony, The Grove Plaza, Boise, June 20, 2015.

Display of African fabrics by Thara Fashions, The Grove Plaza, Boise, June 20, 2015.

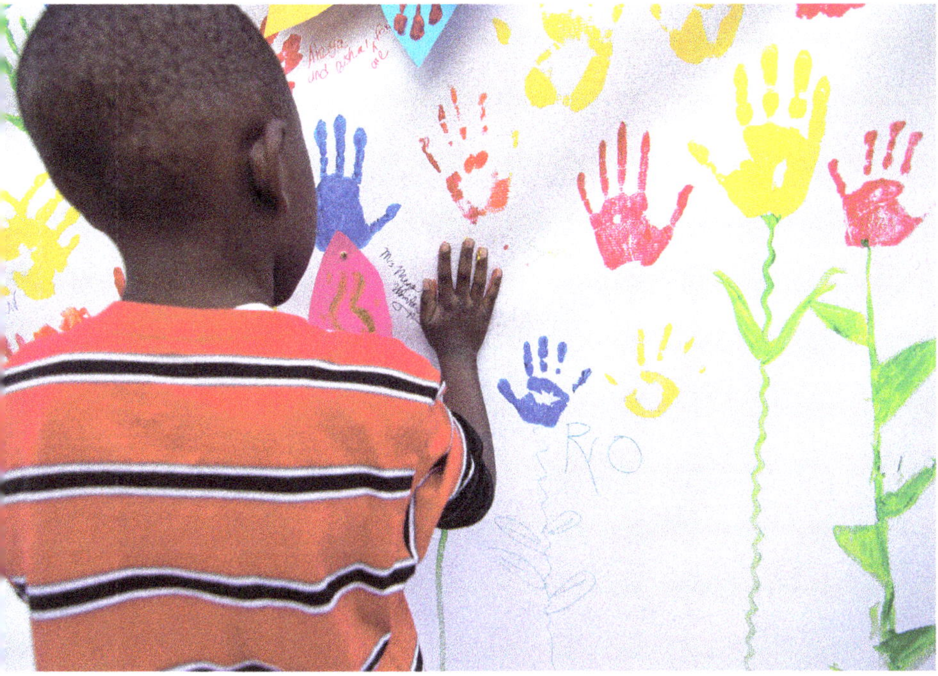

IDAHO OFFICE FOR REFUGEES

"Community Peace" art project by Jessica Miceli-Dodd, Boise City Hall, June 18, 2016.

IDAHO OFFICE FOR REFUGEES

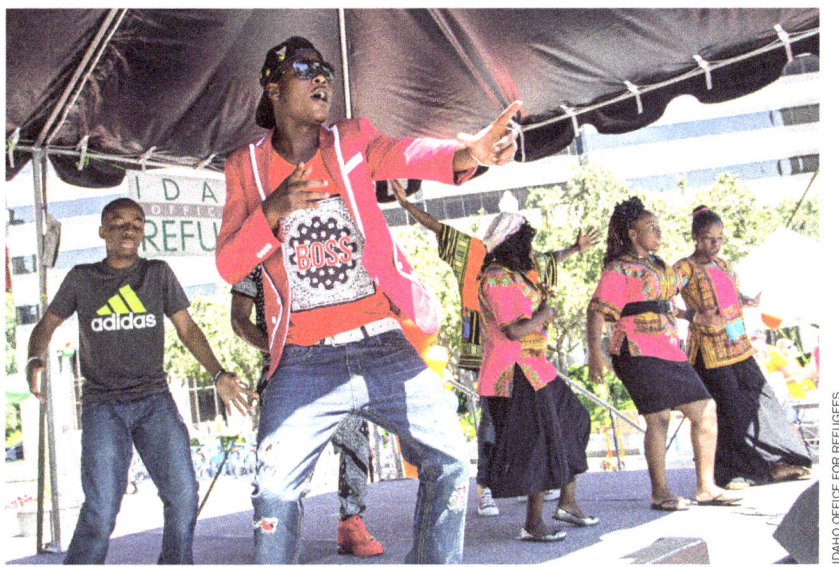

Rocking The Grove Plaza, Boise, June 20, 2015.

Refugee Worldfest Day performance in Brisbane, Australia, 2015.

World Refugee Day Soccer Friendly tournament, Ann Morrison Park, Boise, June 18, 2016.

Global Lounge Group drummer, Ann Morrison Park, Boise, June 18, 2016.

Festival T-shirt, Boise, June 23, 2013.

Celebrating citizenship in Ann Morrison Park, Boise, 2016.

Refugee art day in Amman, Jordan, 2014.

By Katherine Jones

This is a story of refugee kids empowered through soccer, creating their own story of their lives. Playing in Idaho Rush's U-16 coed league, Nations United's first game, as well as their season finale, was against a recreational team from Boise High School, a team that became their nemesis. The journey up to and between those two games is life in a nutshell. It's a story of refugees making their place in a new home; it's a story of kids growing into themselves. It's a story that embraces wins and losses, that cements the correlation between hard work and the payoff. It's the story of a bunch of kids from countries strewn around the world forged into one team – nations, united.

Beginnings

The scene – and it is just that, a scene – at Simplot Fields in southeast Boise is a pretty familiar one for soccer players across the Treasure Valley. On any given Saturday, thousands of uniformed players are scattered across nearly two dozen fields of play. Proud parents take their places along the sidelines; the sounds of laughter and cheers, whistles and shouts waft on the wind. It's a ubiquitous weekend for families. Soccer is a gateway sport, and some of these kids have played since they were 4 years old.

At Field 20 for the first game of the fall 2016 season, however, there was no such feeling of comfort and familiarity. Most of the players from team Nations United had never been to Simplot Fields before. The team is comprised of mostly refugees – from Iraq, Congo, Thailand, Somalia. While some of them had played soccer before, this was their debut as a team and as soccer players American style. For most, this would be their first game – ever – played on a field with grass, stripes, uniforms, referees, and against a team of strangers. Forward Sajjad Al Swaiedi said, "My first real game."

When the referee blew the whistle to start the match, that sound also delineated the moment between "before" and "after." Before, Nations United was just an idea that didn't exist. Before, the notion of a team was merely a pie-in-the-sky dream by some soccer-obsessed kids and a good-hearted teacher. And before, the kids merely chased the ball

around and called it soccer. Sajjad declared, "Now we know how to play like professional. We're like real soccer players."

At South Junior High, the whole school reads every day, anything they want, for 15 minutes, and that's where it all began. Sajjad and classmate Yousif Fartoos, then both eighth-

Sajjad Al Swaiedi, right, and Coach Fawad Saheb-Khan. "We had skills, but we didn't know how to use [them]," says Sajjad. "Then [Coach] showed us the right way. He's a great man. He helps us a lot."

Previous page: Patience Ishimwe cheers for everyone — teammates as well as their competition, the Boise High players — as medals are awarded after the championship game.

graders, lived and breathed soccer. They would pester librarian Mary Karol Taylor for books about anything soccer. Did she have books on certain international players? Like Lionel Messi for Sajjad. Or this team and that team? It's the one sport she can talk about a little because her son has played since he was old enough. He, too, was a Barcelona fan, and through him, she knew some of the players. That was enough to keep the conversation rolling.

She also talked to the boys' teachers about their preoccupation: "[Their teachers] said, 'Oh, every assignment they just try to twist the assignment to be in some way about soccer.'" Every essay, they built it into something about soccer. Poems – how many poems can you write about soccer? Apparently a lot.

When spring rolled around, Taylor's son was excited about the season, so she asked the boys if they were excited to start practice, too. "As it came out of my mouth, I was wishing I could take it back. ... Their response was, 'Yeah, no. We're not on a team.'" At the time, South offered a once-a-week, after-school soccer club, but that's not what Taylor had in mind. These kids were obsessed with soccer, and they weren't on a team.

"I started saying to some of their teachers, 'Let's get them on a team.' When they said, 'Yes, we'll help,' I knew we could do this." It wasn't just Sajjad and Yousif; there was a whole group of refugee kids looking for soccer books. "I said something about: 'Do you wish you could be on a team? Do you want to be on a team?' They said: 'We would love to be on a team – like a real team? We would love to be on a real team.' So I said, 'I'm going to make this happen.' Like, how hard could it be?"

South Junior High School librarian and team founder, Mary Karol Taylor, celebrates the championship win with Su Reh.

Sajjad

Sajjad grew up in Baghdad, the capital city of Iraq. "There is a lot fighting; it's still going on right now. Sometimes I hear – it's an everyday thing, we hear bad news. People get killed; bombs blow up." He said he got used to it. In 2013, when his family left Iraq because his father worked with Americans, he was 12 years old. "For our safety, he wanted a better education for us. The opportunities back there, not very strong for education. I was excited to come [to the U.S.], but still, I know I will miss my family, my grandma, all the people there, my friends, everyone."

In Iraq, Sajjad played soccer in the dirt field behind the mosque. "We had a ball; it was always flat. The goals were like big rocks on two sides. We just played." When it rained, it was mud. Sajjad's mother scolded him for getting dirty. "That was the fun of it. We still went to play. ... [My mom would say,] 'You're going to get sick; it's cold.' I just ignore it."

Arriving in Boise, Sajjad knew a little English: cat, dog, car. Immersion into American life was difficult. "I didn't really go out for one year. For one year, I didn't speak English that much so I just stayed at home." He met Yousif and Justin Karangwa in seventh grade at the Hillside Language Academy. "I didn't have to speak with them English that well; they just play with me;

they understand. Yousif speaks my language, Justin doesn't; but they know me as a friend."

Sajjad's second year in Boise was different. "I spoke English, I came to South, and I had teachers who know about soccer, like Mrs. Taylor." The idea of a team started getting bigger. Taylor told Sajjad his job was to get players. He wanted Yousif on the team. "I said, 'Yousif, help me.' 'Listen,' he said, 'this team is not going to happen.' I just looked at him: 'Don't be negative.' He said, 'Just trust me, it's not going to happen.' I said, 'One day, I'll just remind you of what you say.'"

Organizing

So it was harder than it looked. Organizing a team is a big deal, requiring a great deal of parental involvement, time, money, and commitment – and usually a volunteer parent as coach. A team of refugee students would have none of that support. Their families have no extra money for fees; working (frequently nights) was a priority for parents. Often the family would have only one car, and it wasn't going to be used for schlepping kids to and from practice and games. Language was a barrier, and the culture of parents-on-the-sidelines was neither a priority nor on the radar. It couldn't be by definition.

Taylor explained, "I guess I got really motivated because these kids love soccer so much. I have seen how my son has benefited since he was 5 years old, being part of the soccer community: friendships that he's built, the character he's built by being on team sports. He's just gotten so much out of soccer. I just thought it was sad for [these kids] not to have that kind of experience."

Displaced youth play on a make-shift soccer field, Nyamukwara, Zimbabwe, 2006.

What all of the refugee kids played was street soccer. Survival of the fittest, getting and keeping the ball, scoring as many goals as you can. When Sajjad tried out for the Borah soccer team, for instance (prior to the season with Nations United), he didn't make it – not because he wasn't skilled, but because he didn't know how to play a position and play with a team. These are all things that American youth club soccer players learn from day one.

It wasn't so much that South didn't have an organized team, but if these students didn't learn about positions and

Kyaw Soe, from Thailand, played with Borah Junior Varsity during the season but was invited to play with Nations United after the season ended. "They are my friends," he says. "People from all the cultures, we all meet together on the team."

teamwork, they would never be able to play on high school teams either. This idea of Taylor's was far-reaching. She approached Idaho Rush Soccer Club, which has a long history of helping refugee kids (including 10 years of hosting their One World soccer camp for new refugee kids).

"I said: 'I don't know how; I'm going to try to come up with the money. We won't get a volunteer coach – how much would it cost to get a coach?' ... Once I had that, I knew what I needed to work for. They loved the idea." Rush helped with scholarships for the entire team, but Taylor still had to raise $4,600. A grant from Dick's Sporting Goods cut that in half, and through crowdfunding on a teacher site – with solicits to everyone on Taylor's email list, friends in the soccer community, teachers, a Facebook posting – the team was funded. In less than 24 hours, uniforms, registration fees, and a coach were all paid.

With the score 1-0 in the championship game, the team listens intently as Coach Fawad Saheb-Khan explains the strategy to keep the lead.

The Coach

Coach Fawad Saheb-Khan is himself a refugee, born in Kunduz, Afghanistan. His father moved the family to Pakistan, trying to get to Russia for a better life, but it didn't work out. His father was killed when he went back to Afghanistan to visit – Fawad was very young – and his mother qualified as a refugee. "Going to America, that was all that mattered for us. Nothing mattered about where we were going to go, what part of America we were going to to. That's all we knew, we were coming to America. We didn't know anything about Boise, Idaho; never heard of it before until we actually arrived here."

The first year in Boise was as lonely as Sajjad's. "I was scared the first couple of months. The rumors you hear when you come to a new country – you want to play it safe. There was not a lot of communication because I could not speak the language. I was with a bunch of people who spoke English; I was only a kid just recently moved to America. I started at old East Junior High School.

"When I first started, everybody thought I was Hispanic because of my color of skin and everything. A lot of people who passed me by would say 'Hola,' or another Spanish word, but I didn't understand; I thought it was English, too. Later on, I made some Spanish friends and they were like, 'Oh, we thought you were Spanish; every time we would pass you by, in seventh grade hall, that's why we would say, "Hola." You didn't respond, like, what is wrong with this guy?'

"So I made some friends in junior high, but until my freshman year, I kind of studied and learned the language, worked on my homework. Never got out on my break or recess, never went out to interact. I was focused on learning the language."

Again like Sajjad, Saheb-Khan had always played soccer. "I grew up playing on the streets, barefoot, one soccer ball, 20 people running, no positioning for it – just going after the ball, trying to score. … We would mark the goals with shoes. No experience as far as playing with team, but I kind of developed my skills playing on the streets with friends." A tutor, helping Saheb-Khan with homework, introduced him to American soccer. He started in Rush's select level but had the skills to move up to a traveling competitive team through Rush's scholarship program. All that helped him both socially and linguistically.

"Making more friends, getting to know more people. That was the cool thing. Just learning the language a little faster. Getting out, speaking with people, even if you don't speak [English well]. That kind of helped. My team was super nice; each and every one of them were very nice to me when I played soccer. They would give me a ride if I needed a ride. … At that time, when we first came, there was only one car. I rode my bike most of the time to get from point A to point B." In wintertime, teammates would offer him rides. "They made the transition easier to kind of blend in with them. It wasn't like 'Oh, I'm different.' They were super nice to me actually."

Saheb-Khan made the Timberline soccer team, so he played for both Rush and his school. Word got around. "People knew me: 'Fawad, he's on the soccer team, the varsity team.' I made a bunch of friends just knowing I was on the soccer team. ... [But] when you play a little bit of soccer with other teams that you face and they go to the same school, they go, 'Oh, I remember this guy. Hey, this guy is really good.' They talk about you to other friends – so I made friends like that, also."

After graduation, Saheb-Khan went to College of Western Idaho for a year, continued playing soccer, and got his license to coach in Idaho. He was an assistant coach with a U-13 boys team when the CEO of Idaho Rush Soccer Club, Lee Riley, told him about this fledgling team being started and asked if he'd like to be the head coach. "That kind of opened up the door for me ... make my own decisions, come up with the plans, coach a team the way I wanted to. So, 'Yes, I want to do it.' That's where it started."

Practice

The team, that is, anybody who hoped to be on the team, practiced all summer long. At one point, there were 30 kids on the list. Taylor said, "I wanted to see who was really going to come – who was going to show up and be committed. The team looks really different now than it looked in the beginning. ... When it came down to actually truly practicing and having to come when maybe they didn't want to come, or there was something better to do, some of them just stopped coming and they lost their spot."

By August she said, "It came down to: This is our team. These are our committed kids. Kids who got the spots on the team are kids who came all the time. If they weren't going to come, they let us know; they communicated with us. One of the things I've seen is just understanding the responsibility of what it means to be on a team and not letting your team down. And our coach is expecting you to show up. You can't just not come. That's one huge thing."

Coach Fawad worked the kids hard, and it must be noted, he wasn't paid for summer coaching. He held a weeklong conditioning camp, had them run a mile in the hot sun, do drill after drill after drill. He coached during Ramadan, the

Muslim holy month that includes fasting from dawn till sunset. Sajjad said, "I was fasting one of the months, but I still showed up. Coach was fasting, and he still showed up and did OK. If he shows up, why can't I? ... The love of the game kept me going."

There were other challenges as well. Taylor said, "At one point, I was going to figure out how to get them cleats and shin guards. ... I ended up deciding that was something they had to do. They had to figure that out. They had to talk to their families. They needed to invest in something. ... So they somehow borrowed them, found them." The kids had to learn it wasn't good enough just to show up to practice. They had to show up in cleats, in shin guards, wearing a white shirt, and with a ball. "We're still struggling with the balls. They pop, they lose them, some kids never did get a ball. I just said, 'It's the rules.'"

Nations United's very first game ended in a tie, which the team — including Pit Poe, left, and Ehpaw Ku — considered as good as a win.

But the most momentous lesson that summer, far and away what made the most lasting impression on the kids, was playing positions. Sajjad said: "How to play position and how to move on the field. I didn't know that in the beginning. I just had skills, nothing more than that. It's a big field, 11 players. Each player has to play a certain spot and move in a certain way. I learned about that. That was the biggest thing about the summer."

Coach Fawad said: "When I first picked them up for their first practice, there were 20, 30 people running for one ball. When I picture it, that was myself. The same thing I did with a bunch of my friends."

Prisca Hermene, left, from Congo; Sajjad Al Swaiedi from Iraq; and Claude Chimemana from Congo, center, gather for the team cheer: "Nations United!"

Sajjad said: "It was big for our team's defenders, too. They have really big parts to do. They're defenders, they have lots of pressure on them. It is one of the things they had to learn. The whole team learned something during the summer. They learned many things, not just something. We became more of a team instead of individuals. That's how we work."

Playing positions was like a key that unlocked a treasure. And so, one Saturday in September, the kids piled into a van – another arrangement Taylor made, this time with Boise

City Parks and Recreation – and headed out to Simplot Fields to put it to the test.

First Game

The teams couldn't have been much different. The Boise High team was experienced, confident, and, by all accounts, really good. Nations United was nervous, tentatively confident, and unknown. But when both teams took the field, there was only one language: soccer.

Nancy Henderson is a critical reading and writing teacher at South. She and other teachers filled out the sidelines in place of parents who couldn't be there. Henderson said: "[Nearly] every team they played the first time they [beat], and they won handily, because nobody thought they were going to be good because of who they were. Once they understood these kids knew how to play soccer – they may not know all the rules, they've never played on a club, they've never played with refs, they've never played with nets. But they know how to play and they don't give up.

"The second time they played them it's like, 'Whoa, we've got to take these guys seriously.'"

Sajjad also remembered his promise. "I just gave it to him: 'Yousif, remember those three months ago? Remember what you said?' He said, 'Ah, yeah.' 'Like, it happened. I told you it was going to happen and it happened. ... Just being positive makes it easy.'"

Their first game ended in a hard-fought tie, 1-1. For Nations United, it was as good as a win. Sajjad beamed, "Now we know how to play like professional. We're like real soccer players. [Coach said] we look like a real team. We all know our positions." Sajjad had always said his biggest dream was to play a game with referees. "And that came true. I played many, like eight games, with refs and stuff. It felt like a real game – there's grass, goalkeepers, possession; we got the real hard ball, like size 5, and like 11 people [on the team], a bench, coaches – it's real. Grass to play on, not mud. It's real. Everything was real."

Sajjad reflected, "My first real game. It was better than I expected."

Prisca Hermene hugs teammate and friend Ehpaw Ku before a practice.

A Loss

The season progressed. After the tie with Boise, Nations United beat Arsenal and Timberline, and played Boise High again, losing by one point. Then, on one double-header Saturday, missing three key players and some girls (which limited the possibilities for substitutions), Nations United lost 0-4 to Boise High. It was a bitter loss.

Between games, they went to Whitney Community Center for lunch. Taylor said, "Ehpaw wouldn't get out of the van. She played defender. She was so upset and crying, felt so awful and that she had let the team down. Eh Doh (the goalie) – the same thing. He just sat down ... in my car. ... He just pulled his jersey over his face and just sobbed. Just had to let it out."

After a miserable lunch, Sajjad gathered the players together. He recounts the moment: "Our goalkeeper got humiliated the most because they score on him. He feels really bad, started crying. I had to do my best to get him back up. Not just me – the whole team was trying their best to get him back up. Like it's not your fault, we should have helped you.

"I say to them, 'It's not your fault we lost. We are a team. We lose as a team and win as a team. It's not one individual problem.' They keep blaming themselves. It wouldn't help because we already lost that game. 'Let's talk forward to the next one. ... We got another game. [To the goalie], it's not your fault. I should have helped you, the defenders should have helped you. It's not all about you. Leave it, look to the next game.' I said, 'I promise you I'll do my best not to let them close to you.' He just stopped [crying] and we were talking and everything was good. Better. He start believing in himself."

They gathered around the pool table and everybody put their hands in for Nations United. They got on the bus and went back to the field. "The next game, [the goalie] saved really hard shots. The defenders were really protecting him, trying their best not to get any score on it. We tied that game and Coach said, 'See? That's the way we should have played in the beginning.'"

Lessons of Soccer

If you ask the kids what they learned over the course of Nations United's season, there is a consistent refrain: "I learned to play position." But with an adult-size perspective, clearly they've learned more. Much more. Henderson pointed out: "I think what I've noticed most is they've developed a real camaraderie with everybody. They're friends now, where they hadn't really known each other before. They all take pride in what they're doing, but they take pride in other people as well. And to see them at school, you just see the confidence. You see them take ownership of their learning; you see them know that they're as good as any of the kids there."

Taylor, in particular, has looked for the correlation between soccer and scholarship; it helps build a case should she want to tackle funding for year two of Nations United. "The [English Language Learner] teacher said the teamwork that they've built on the soccer team has transferred over into the classroom. They had some group project and their group was the first one done; it was all done correctly. ... The other thing, [a couple of the kids] said that all these teachers are telling them, 'Congratulations,' and 'Good job.' "

Taylor added: "I just can't see how it doesn't help in their school. I think they feel so much more confident and connected, with not only just each other but staff. It was on the school announcements that they won the championship, and they felt so proud."

Yousif Fartoos was one of the soccer-obsessed students who motivated South Junior High School librarian Mary Karol Taylor to found Nations United. "When I came to the team," he says, "I found new friends. We have fun. We get better at soccer."

Sajjad says that when he has good games and good practices, his mind feels open. Taylor said: "I just believe so strongly that when kids feel connected to something, they do better in school. Hopefully, too, there's some transference: When they work hard, it pays off. And when there's a failure, you don't just quit, you keep working. ... Try harder, do better, have more grit, stick with things."

One day not long after their first game, Sajjad and Yousif wandered into Amber Strickler's classroom where they had written all their poems about soccer. It took a while for them to come to the point, but what they were shyly hoping was that they could get copies of the photos she had taken at the game.

Taylor explained: "Well, come to find out – now that my son has connected with them on social media – they all have pictures of them in their Rush jerseys on their profile pictures. It's giving them an identity. An identity and something to belong to. We all want to belong to something. … Rush Soccer Club is huge. You've been out there, seen all the kids wearing Rush jerseys. And now they are, too."

Team and Community

When refugees finally, finally get to come to America, the challenges don't magically disappear. Taylor said: "It's not easy. It's a hard thing for them when they come here and they realize they're working nights, they don't get to see their family; families are all over the place because everyone's just trying to make ends meet. They don't have the larger support of a community; they don't have all the aunts and uncles and cousins they maybe had back in their home country. It's hard.

"It's great for the Boise community to step up. And so many people step up in so many ways. To not only get them set up, but to [help them] feel really connected and fit in, to find a place and belong." Taylor is not the only one giving her time and energy to Nations United way beyond the scope of librarian. "There's a lot of awesome, generous people who want to help refugees fit into our community. If we are not embracing them in our community, it's our loss."

Besides the support of Rush, other folks have pitched in. For the time between double-header games, teachers at South passed around a sign-up sheet and provided lunch. When Henderson wrote to her son – a goalie on an adult team in the Bay Area – that Nations United's goalie didn't have any gloves, he sent a pair, and then he sent a pair of pants and a goalie jersey as well. "That's kind of what you're supposed to do," she said.

Henderson added: "What it's going to do for a lot of them is [give them] the sense that they can accomplish things, that America really is the land to be in, that there is a future, that there are possibilities here, and that they can be treated as an equal. I think that's really important for these kids to understand: That they really are going to become ... a part of American culture."

Forward Hamsa Jama said: "I am feeling American. Before, a refugee still. Now we're not."

Taylor said: "So the first team picture we took – for a lot of them, it's on their Facebook page. It's like: Here's what I'm part of. Their main Facebook photo is of the team. They belong."

Justin Karangwa, center, and the United Nations bench cheer from the sidelines during the U-16 coed end-of-season tournament.

Final Game of the Season

Nations United ended their season 5-3 with their share of victories and losses. The championship tournament was over the course of three days. They won one game, tied one game, and on Friday night, they lost to rival Boise High 0-4. However, they still had the second-best U-16 coed record, so Saturday's game was a rematch: No. 1, Boise High vs. No. 2, Nations United. Sajjad said: "Coach just like, 'Believe in me, believe. Believe in yourself. We got this again.'"

For a tense first half, no one scored, although there were plenty of attempts. Both teams were determined, skilled, and disciplined. Nations United had several shots on goal, but they were too far out. And then midway into the second half,

Sandrine Niyonsenga, right, gives in to emotional tears after the championship game. She is hugged by Patience Ishimwe, center, and Prisca Hermene.

Hamsa Jama did exactly what his coach told him to do: He got closer to the goal – and scored. The final minutes were agonizing with Coach Fawad orchestrating defensive strategies that players executed on the field. That positions thing.

Coach Fawad said: "It helps you to know what is your purpose. What is your goal, what do you want to accomplish in this position? Before, [when I was a kid], I thought my purpose was to help my team everywhere I could go. But they have their part that they have to do; your job is to do this part and make sure that part is done correctly for you. Everything else would come. Trusting."

When the whistle blew to end the game, it marked another "before" and "after:" Team Nations United were champions. Players on the field ran to the bench, and the bench stormed the field, cheering worthy of a World Cup victory. Sajjad proclaimed, "This is more important to me than the World Cup." Everyone hugged, and jumped, and screamed. Sajjad ripped off his shirt. Tears were shed.

Coach Fawad said: "The team has come a long way for being first time, playing in any team. I didn't win a

Team Nations United surrounds Coach Farad Saheb-Khan for a team cheer after the championship medals are passed out.

championship on my first-ever team playing." He laughs now, but he struggled to hold back tears then. "I was emotional actually. I'm kind of tough, trying to tough it up, not to show it. [But] the reason I was emotional was because everything that they win, through each and every game, I was there to see them."

Prisca Hermene joined the team a little late. Taylor found her during one game cheering on the sidelines for her friends on the field, and the team was desperate for girls. Prisca said: "There's a reason for every single opportunity that comes up in your life and you should definitely – whatever chance you have – take it. Take it because you never know what could happen.

"That's the same thing with the world. Even if it's scary. I was scared [watching that first game]. They looked so good ... and I was like, I don't think I can, I don't think I'm as good. And at the end of it, having a medal that says you're a champion. And you did it. You helped the team win, and you were a part of it. That's so amazing."

Future Dreams

Basketball starts soon and then track in the spring. According to Henderson: "A lot of them want to play basketball. I think a lot of them, especially the really fast boys, are going to try out for track, which is going to make our track team incredible. [They learned] the confidence to be in an American sport ... and then to be able to go on to play the other sports that they want to. ... It's also going to teach them to work in groups of people that they don't already know.

Forward Hamsa Jama is honored with the golden shoe and "the most incredible goal" award by Coach Fawad Saheb-Khan, left, and Mary Karol Taylor. Hamsa scored the only — and winning — goal in the championship game.

It's going to give them a sense of what a team is and how American sports are: They're not for just insiders, they're for everybody.

"And just because you can't go to the [sports] camps and you didn't go to the camps when you were 4 or 5 years old, or you haven't played it all your life, you can still pick it up. You can still go; you can still try."

Spring soccer starts, too. And then there's the fall season when many of the older kids will try out for the high school soccer teams. It will be bittersweet to leave Nations United if there is a second year, but there's also a sense of urgency.

Sajjad pointed out: "To be able to get a college scholarship or professional team scholarship, they come and see you at a high school game or practice and they see how good you do. That's how they take professional players. So I have to get on a high school team." It is clear to each of the members of Nations United: Sports is a way to college. Sports offers the opportunity for scholarships to pay for tuition that none of their families can afford.

Sajjad said: "I came here to really get a better education. A better life and an education. In order to become a better person, you got to get to the college." And for those who dream really, really big, playing sports in college is a way to be discovered for professional teams. Defender Claude Chimemana said: "What I think in my life in the future, if I keep playing soccer, I will be a good guy like this. ... I think I am going to help a lot of people when I am rich because of the sports I play. I am going to help my country. Like the refugees who live in Africa, I can go back and help them."

When Taylor set out to find Sajjad and Yousif a soccer team to play on, it was simply because they loved soccer so much. "My son gets to do that. Just by luck of his birth, he gets to play soccer and have this huge, full life of team sports and these kids don't. Maybe they're not the best players to get everybody's attention, but they have passion for the game and they want to play – and they should be able to. That was a big thing that motivated me."

Through Nations United the door to opportunities might be opening. These kids have done more than play soccer, they've excelled. And possibly it's not just soccer that they've excelled at, or that they will excel at. Taylor said: "Maybe Sajjad won't become a pro soccer player, but hopefully ... he became empowered. He experienced that with perseverance you can make something happen in your life. Yeah, I raise money and drive them around and get other people in our community to notice them, but all that is just to give them a little boost. ... Coach Fawad and all these kids took this team on with commitment. They are the ones who decided to all work together despite the fact that the boys weren't thrilled in the beginning to play with girls; despite the fact that they all were just learning English; and [despite the fact] that they didn't have parents who were figuring all this out for them.

"They decided to figure out how to get cleats, how to get a bike to get to practice. They decided they wanted to all become friends and support one another. They decide they wanted to respect and listen to their coach and support him – even if he made them run or do the bear crawl because they weren't listening to him. Maybe other kids would've just walked away, thinking he was too hard on them."

At Whitney Community Center, Nations United team members hang decorations for a post-season awards ceremony and potluck dinner celebration.

The kids really didn't have much to lose by walking away from Taylor's rules or Coach Saheb-Khan's hard practices. They didn't pay to be on the team, and their parents most likely wouldn't have made them stay. "They really are writing their own story," says Taylor. "Coach Fawad too – at 23, he is a kid himself – with his [life] all ahead of him still. ... We like to think that everyone in America can 'write their own story.' But we know some are more empowered than others."

Only time will tell how a search for soccer books and a persistent librarian will have changed the course of individual lives – and perhaps of the world. Sajjad imagines how this soccer season will look to him 20 years from now: "It's going to play a big part. It's going to become a story how I once came into the library, asked for books; that teacher, she tried her best. I'm really thankful to her. Right now, I'm really thankful she got me on a team. It's going to become something big, a big part of my life. ... In 20 years, I don't know where I'll get; we'll see. But it started here. It all started here."

Sajjad Al Swaiedi thanks Coach Fawad Saheb-Khan at the awards ceremony, a fitting end to the fall season.

KATHERINE JONES is an award-winning photojournalist for the *Idaho Statesman*, the state's largest newspaper.

7 | Policing Softly

Boise police nurture community.

By Chelsee Boehm

Laws emerge from customs, traditions, and norms. But things Americans take for granted can bewilder people from distant places, and that confusion can lead to terror for people displaced by violence and war. Even routine encounters with law enforcement – a traffic stop, a parking citation – can be terrifying. Without nuanced communication in a common language, there is seldom a foundation of trust.

"Police cars can look intimidating to someone who has been traumatized," says officer Dustin Robinson of the Boise Police Department, "and the same thing goes with the uniform. It looks paramilitaristic."

Robinson, an 8-year veteran, is proud to serve as the department's refugee liaison. Friendly but tough-looking with a shaved head and trim goatee, the policeman does what he can to soften his appearance. He holsters his Glock under his sport coat. He drives an unmarked police car. He relies on interpreters and plenty of patience to solve problems and establish rapport.

The low-key approach is well-suited to a refugee resettlement city. It is also a tribute to a 20-year national trend. Community-oriented policing, now an office of the U.S. Justice Department, became a cornerstone of Clinton-era criminal justice reform. In Boise after seven police shooting incidents in the late 1990s, city council hired a citizen-police ombudsman and took community policing to heart. Gradually the emphasis shifted from confrontation to prevention and education. Foot patrols, a police dog mascot, milk-and-cookie sessions with children, meet-and-greets on Main Street, and dozens of partnership programs were part of the transformation. So was an initiative to cope with Boise's coming-of-age as a refugee resettlement hub.

Officer Shelli Sonnenberg pioneered the liaison program. Established in 2006 and housed in the department's Community Outreach Division, the liaison at first was chiefly concerned with barriers that prevented refugees from reporting a crime. "We didn't know crime was occurring," Sonnenberg says, recalling the challenge. "In some of the cultures, for example the Somali-Bantu community, the elders took care of the

Community policing relies on partnerships that build on a foundation of trust.

Previous page: Dustin Robinson, Boise Police Department's refugee liaison, 2016.

problems. It wasn't a police matter." Police needed that cultural context. Refugees, in turn, needed to know that police could do more than enforce.

"Law enforcement isn't just about making an arrest," says Robinson, who became the liaison when Sonnenberg made detective. In 2016 city historian Chelsea Boehm sat down with Sonnenberg and Robinson for her master's research project on community policing. The interviews, excerpted herein, have been edited for length and clarity. Full transcripts are available in research archives maintained by the Boise City Department of Arts and History.

Chelsee Boehm: Detective Sonnenberg, you served as the refugee and immigrant liaison from 2006 to 2012. How did the program come about?

Shelli Sonnenberg: Most refugees, when they first came over, were living in apartment complexes. We noticed an increase in [minor] theft, such as lawn ornaments and bicycles. Some refugees, I learned, came from camps where anything of importance was kept inside. Well, in the U.S., we leave plants out. We leave chairs out. We leave bicycles out. We leave things like wind chimes out for decoration. Refugees sometimes thought those outside items were things people did not want. We realized that it was better to educate than write people up.

I thought it might be best if a single officer dealt with those specific issues. I wrote up a proposal and brought it to the command staff. There were many civilians who worked with refugees, but no police department had a sworn officer who was dedicated to working with that population.

Detective Shelli Sonnenberg, 2012

Who were your sponsors and partners?

SS: I met with the Idaho Office for Refugees, Agency for New Americans, and World Relief. I reached out to the BSU department of social work. I met with Warm Springs Counseling. When the IRC (International Rescue Committee) came to Boise, I brought them on board as well. We used the [Jannus] English Language Center for two-hour classes that taught refugees the law. We started with simple things like how to cross a street.

Officer Robinson hands out frozen treats at World Refugee Day, 2016.

We made mistakes, at first, mostly because of regulations we've put in place ourselves. In the early years when we were bringing in Bosnians and Serbo-Croatians, we put them in the same apartment complexes and schools. War [between them] has gone on for thousands and thousands of years that we, as Americans, don't understand, and we've put their enemy right next door. There was fear of the police. We had no way of knowing who was a refugee and where they were from. Fair housing issues made it hard to ask about nationality. [That problem] opened the door to good conversations with Idaho Housing.

Once the communication opened, our network expanded quickly. I can remember going to an apartment complex where refugees had quit flushing the toilet because it had overflowed once. They did not tell anybody, so the overflow damaged the neighbor's apartment below. When the apartment manager told the [refugee] tenants that they needed to report things, the refugees heard something different. They thought they would be kicked out if the toilet overflowed, so they quit flushing it. So, again, it was a matter of education.

How did refugees respond to the police liaison?

SS: I am guessing from their point of view, many of them probably are like, "Okay, so where's the hitch?" We really created the position as we went, not knowing how best to present it. I spent a lot of time going out to picnics and educational trainings. "If you have a question, call me," I told them.

Domestic battery was really difficult. I made sure I explained everything ahead of time. If something happens and there is evidence, police have to act. But sometimes, not always, but sometimes, I could educate people in American

The American system of criminal justice can baffle and frustrate newly arrived refugees.

terms. We could communicate [indirectly] by saying, "I have a friend who ... ." You know how that happens, right? Sometimes we [hypothetically] worked through the problem. "If this were to happen, this would happen." It was information they could take back to their "sister" or "friend." We also worked with case managers saying, "This is what you need to tell your client." We tried to be very careful with confidentiality issues.

Did refugees have fearful preconceptions about what American police might be like?

SS: I think that was a huge issue, and then on top of that I was a woman, right? [Laughs.] So there's a lot of corruption, a lot of fear, a lot of bribing that goes on in many of these other countries. There were offers to bribe when the Bosnians first got here. That's how the police functioned over there. Burmese and the Nepali are fearful because over there you never barter with police. You just do what they said. For the Burundis, the Congolese, and the Somali-Bantu, that uniform was absolutely frightening.

I used to teach the refugee class in full uniform. I knew that I wasn't getting through to them, but when I walked into one of the agencies and somebody that I had had in the class, I could tell their reaction was different. I wasn't quite so scary. Even if I did have a gun on my hip, the uniform, I think, was getting in the way of communicating. [People were] wondering if I am going to arrest them, take them away, or even kill them. So that was one of the first things that I changed.

Badges of authority can intimidate and complicate refugee outreach.

Sometimes I would bring in a [policeman in a] uniform and ask, "How many times have you shot somebody?" The officer would say, "None." And then I would explain that sometimes we have to pull our gun, but we don't want to hurt anybody. It was not an easy process. We made mistakes. I just want to go back to some of them from the early days and go, "I am sorry, we were doing our best!" [Laughs.]

I can remember when a large Iraqi population arrived, and they were voting on who they were going to appoint to their association. I asked if I could attend the meeting. I sat in the back [in case they had questions]. Having some of the elders ask questions, I think, made it okay for the other people to ask questions. And the funny thing was that the questions they asked are what anybody would ask. "I have four kids," someone would say. "How am I going to support them?" None of the questions were weird.

Officer volunteers at Boise Bicycle Project, 2016.

How did you work to change their perceptions?

SS: Sometimes it was just a matter of making a little effort. I was involved in a program called Kids' Corner. The refugees, when they first get here they get their first shots, but there's a lot of follow up shots. Kids' Corner was a program where Central District Health and the Boise Police Department came together, and we took out a mobile van and went to the

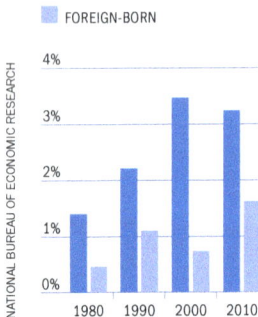

U.S. Incarceration Rates of Men Age 18-39, by Nativity, 1980-2010

apartment complexes, went door-to-door in the morning and then offered shots in the afternoon to get the people who maybe were unaware that there's follow-up shots for immunization or weren't able to pay for them.

I actually did a health and safety check when refugees were resettled. If there were little kids in the house, I would show them plastic plugs to cover the outlets. So, even though I was a police officer, refugees began to learn that I was there to make them safe.

As you taught refugees about Boise, did they teach you as well?

SS: The job taught me patience. America is very time-driven. "I'll meet with you at 10:00 tomorrow," I'd say, but they only heard "tomorrow," meaning "anytime." In the beginning, it was hard to stay on track. I learned to call the night before and even call in the morning and say, "You need to get on that bus today by 8:00, or you're not going to be here at 10:00."

The job also taught me about other cultures and religions. Growing up in Idaho, when I was in high school, it seemed everybody looked just like me. Nowadays, when you walk down the street, you see diversity. It's amazing. It's encouraged me to get out of my little bubble. I can never tell you that I understand the wars and the fighting, but I know that they occur. I have more compassion. I am amazed by the resiliency and selflessness people have for their families. The job helped me see what's important.

Officer Dustin Robinson, you became the refugee and immigrant liaison after six years with the Boise police in 2012. How did you become a policeman?

Dustin Robinson: I grew up in southeastern Idaho in a small farming and ranching community. My mother was a school teacher and my father was a school psychologist, so I always knew that I wanted to be involved in the community. I wanted to be able to work in a field that had a lot of variety to it, but when I went home at the end of the day, or when I looked back at the end of the career, I would be able to say that I made a difference in my community. Prior to the Boise

Police Department, I worked for the Boise County Sheriff's Department. I did that for two and a half years and then made the transition down to Boise City Police Department.

How smooth was the transition from patrol officer to refugee liaison?

DR: As much as I tried to make it seamless, it had some bumps. Just because someone moves thousands of miles across an ocean doesn't mean they leave behind the scars of trauma and the culture they grew up with. [I needed] to grow as a police officer and a human being, to slow down and learn to include those other cultures.

Celebrating refugee day at Boise City Hall, 2016.

[Many refugees] have never been able to trust law enforcement. They don't understand due process. I'm someone they know and can reach out to. I spend time working within the community to get information that might be relevant to other people's safety. So they may give me information if there is arguments or children misbehaving or parents disciplining children as they would have in their own countries, possibly not realizing that that it is illegal in the United States and in the state of Idaho.

Over the last year and a half, we've had delegations from Europe come to study our program in Boise. They come to learn how we educate refugees, what tools do we use to prevent crimes from occurring. I have even had members from other police departments come up and job shadow for a couple days to learn what we are doing.

Officer Robinson, right, greets an Iraqi refugee at his small grocery store in Boise, 2016.

What are some of the biggest challenges?

DR: One of the biggest is having refugees understand that they can turn to law enforcement for service and assistance if they're the victims of crimes. That's difficult to do because they come with years or generations of seeing family members abused by people in power. It is hard to let that fear and trauma go. We've put a lot of positive steps in place to break down those barriers and build trust.

Another challenge is helping individuals learn how our criminal justice process works. Our criminal justice tries to make sure individuals are treated fairly, and that can be slow. It can be confusing and frustrating. We have reassured individuals that something is still happening even if it is not happening quickly.

It takes patience. Different cultures have vastly different beliefs on marriages and family structure. It's not law enforcement's job to force someone to believe in our customs. It is law enforcement's job to make sure that people follow the rules. We have to allow individuals the freedom to express themselves as long as it falls within the laws.

Can you give an example of something illegal in Boise that might be legal somewhere else?

DR: Our driving laws are very strict. Other countries may have traffic laws that are not written down or not strictly enforced. In Boise, even if no one is coming, you can't just drive through a stoplight. How individuals get pulled over for a traffic stop is very different in other parts of the world. We have to teach refugees how to pull a car over and what to do when they get pulled over.

Parenting can also be different in the United States. What is considered child abuse here may be a common form of child discipline in another country.

What have you learned about policing from working with refugees?

DR: I am extremely patriotic. I never thought I took that for granted, but working with individuals from deplorable conditions really makes you appreciate what we have. I have also learned that just because we have done something in our culture for many years doesn't mean that it is the only right way to do something. There are many ways to be good neighbors. Refugees often have strong connections to their communities. In cultures with limited technology, human connections are more important than I had previously realized.

CHELSEE BOEHM holds a master's degree in applied history from BSU. An employee with the Boise City Department of Arts & History, she specializes in oral history and museum work. Todd Shallat contributed to this chapter.

Verse: *Blue*

By Ruby McCarter and Daniah Kadhim

"What is your favorite color?"

This is a game.
Correctly move the pieces,
Correctly arrange the right words
In the right order in your foreign mouth,
And you'll get wide grins, baby talk, praise,
And the title of a refugee.
But you are not a refugee.
That word is broken, used, worn,
And reeks of pity.
You are an immigrant,
Forced by parents to abandon the place
You once called home.

Referred to as
"She",
"That kid",
"It",
Because your name does not roll
Smoothly off the tongue
Like your white sisters, Lucy or Paige.
But do not envy them; you are your people's legacy
And you are more than they know.

They stick you in their stereotypical box,
Telling you,

It is such a shame that you live in a land of terrorists,
Your women are married off young,
You cannot speak your mind.
But that is all they know of your people,
That is all they expect.

You itch to tell them the stories of your ancestors,
That they are human too,
But your words collide and mix
From the journey of your brain to your mouth,
And they watched you with expectant smiles,
Eyes wide with curiosity,
Trying to help, but not knowing how.

Your parents led you here,
With promises of going back.
Even after seeing your white hot fear,
Your quaking anger,
Your tears,
You were still led away
From the generation of your roots.
Here, it's a game.
People bounce you about.
Expect you to adapt,
To say your words right,

To know where the bathroom is
On the first day of school,
When you can't even remember
The teacher's English name.
You have been gone so long that you are afraid
That when you board that plane to go back
The turbulence of your flight will uproot you with the truth,
That you are no longer sure which place is foreign,
And which place is home.

But you cannot tell any of them this.
Your mouth won't let you.
So instead, you shift your grin,
And remember your favorite color.

"Blue."

Makiwa Nduwimana, 18, at the Centennial High School prom, 2016.

From *Nyumbani Means Home: A Collection of Collaborative Poetry* (2015).
RUBY MCCARTER, pictured, attends Boise High School.
DANIAH KADHIM immigrated from a refugee camp in Jordan.

8 | Hidden, Silent, Confused

A survivor negotiates Boise and adolescence.

By Belma Sadikovic with Todd Shallat

On January 7, 1993, a cold Thursday evening, Belma Sadikovic escaped the Bosnian war. She was 9 years old at the time. Her elementary school had been shelled. Her father had been drafted. Fleeing north with her mother via Croatia and Slovenia, she reached Stuttgart, Germany, taking refuge in the home of her aunt. Two years later, the family was reunited. In December 2000, with help from relief agencies and American sponsors, they crossed the Atlantic, reaching Boise by way of New York.

Ethnically, Sadikovic is Bosniak. More fundamentally, in her memory and mind, she is a survivor and a refugee. Sadikovic now teaches education to college students in Boise and Nampa. An emerging scholar, she is a passionate advocate for refugees on a local and global scale. A naturalized citizen, she recently finished her doctoral dissertation in the College of Education at Boise State.

Where are you from? What do you recall of your childhood flight from the war?

I was born in Zenica [now a regional capital city of the Federation of Bosnia and Herzegovina. It is about 40 miles north of Sarajevo].

For the first six years of my life, my parents and I lived in an apartment overlooking the city. We lived with my grandparents, which is common in our culture. My grandmother raised me since both my parents were busy working full-time jobs. My father worked as a master electrician at Željezara Zenica, the biggest steel factory in Bosnia. My mom was the assistant director of Utok, a Slovenian upscale boutique, which served the affluent population in Bosnia prior to war. We lived a very good life prior to the war in Bosnia. We owned an apartment, had a nice car, and spent our summer vacations on the Adriatic Sea. I had a very happy childhood. Then in 1992 the war took everything we had.

The war in Bosnia started on April 6, 1992. After almost a year, my mother and I were fortunate to escape its horrors. On January 7, 1993, when I was 9, my father

paid a stranger his life savings to send my mother and me to live with an aunt in Stuttgart, Germany. The man drove a white Volkswagen hatchback. My father couldn't come with us as he was drafted into the army. We finally reunited in Germany in the summer of 1995. On December 16, 2000, after a year of waiting in Split, Croatia, we flew to Amsterdam and took a connecting flight to New York. We traveled with other refugees –

Sadikovic, age 3, poses below her family's apartment in Bosnia's Zenica, 1988.

Previous page: Belma Sadikovic, 2013.

all easy to identify. We all carried large white bags labeled IOM (International Organization for Migration). I still have our bag.

I also carried a blue backpack filled with goodbye letters and memorabilia given to me by my friends. There were memories and good-luck tokens. I still have everything tucked in my closet, including the backpack and a diary-like notebook, which I only recently started reading. It took much time and effort to compile enough emotional strength to be able to dive back into the raw realities of my experiences as a child refugee.

Our trip to the United States was very intense for my parents and me. The fact that we were crossing the Atlantic Ocean and heading to live on a different continent made us anxious. Furthermore, we had never been on an airplane. I was terrified. But in New York, as we boarded a flight for Denver, I remember the smile of a young TSA officer. "Welcome," he said. My heart grew three sizes.

In Boise we were met by my uncle and his family, who had come to the U.S. two years before. They were our sponsors. Our resettlement caseworker from the Agency for New Americans also greeted us.

Left: Zenica, an industrial hub on the Bosna River.

Right: Southbound highway to Sarajevo.

What was it like to start over in Boise?

In Boise I did not start school again for several months. In a different situation, I would have been thrilled to not be held accountable for going to school. But not this time. At age 16 I had already missed too much school, which created a gap in my education. Instead I accompanied my parents because, although my English was broken, I spoke better than they did. I was responsible for translating.

Our caseworker with the Agency for New Americans spent over a month trying to find an affordable apartment. Meantime we stayed with our sponsors. Affordable housing was hard to find. Not many property owners wanted much to do with refugees. We found an apartment complex on 29th Street that housed other Bosnians and refugees.

I remember our first shopping trip to Winco. The streets seemed so wide; the buildings appeared so big. Winco was filled with different varieties of chips. There was an aisle completely dedicated to soda! And another filled with candy and chocolate! I was in heaven.

We survived on food stamps until my parents found jobs. Two months into our resettlement in Boise, my parents took the first jobs that the caseworker found for them. We did not own a car. My parents walked to work. At times, my mother would get a ride home from one of her co-workers because their shifts would end close to midnight. None of us spoke much English.

Like all refugees during the initial months of resettlement, my family and I underwent medical examinations. We had to complete legal paperwork before I could be enrolled in school. At first I was placed directly in a language academy for newly arrived refugee students. The English Language Academy was housed in Riverglen Junior High, but the refugee kids did not interact with the regular students. We had our own small part of the building downstairs. It felt strange to not be able to go on lunch breaks with the American kids at the same time. It felt humiliating. We felt like outcasts. Isolated, we called our school "the ghetto."

I spent an academic year with my peers in that ghetto until my English was said to be "good enough."

Describe Boise High School. What were your expectations?

My first day in a real American high school was in February 2002, a week before I turned 18. Boise High seemed like a set from a movie. Like the movies I had watched in Germany – films like *Stand and Deliver*, *Clueless*, and *Dangerous Minds* – American students seemed bold and violent, their schools dramatic and cruel.

My first day at Boise High was in the middle of the spring semester. I stared at the floor of my classroom. In my dreams

High school movies like *Clueless* (1995) distort a young refugee's expectations.

TV GUIDE

Zahraa Naser, 18, sitting center in a red hijab, struggles to connect with American classmates at Boise High School, 2016. Naser and her sister, standing left, reached Boise from Syria after her father was killed in Iraq.

I still relive that day. Shoved into the room by a counselor. Avoiding the stares of my classmates. The teacher's high-pitched voice. Introducing myself to the class. My accent was British, having learned choppy English in Germany.

My survival method was to dissociate from who I was and what had happened to me. I would not talk about it. Constant and unexpected traumas and changes prevented me from making genuine human connections. I remained skeptical and reserved. My refugee survival skills helped and hindered: they helped me cope with being an outsider, but they hindered my self-awareness of who I really was.

Did the refugee experience color your education? Your capacity to learn?

I didn't want to stand out. I wanted to fit in. I just wanted to belong. A few months passed. I tried to stay under the radar as much as possible, pretending to be a thinker just so I didn't have to speak English.

As you can imagine, flying under the radar didn't fly with my English teacher. I was placed in a study skills class where I met Mr. Bradberry. Not wanting to mispronounce his name with my British accent, I called him Mr. B. He saw my strengths and became my mentor. He was someone I could talk to and trust. He helped me gain confidence in speaking and writing English. Academically he helped me excel. I became "student of the quarter," although cultural anxieties still held me back.

Students learn compassion for the foreign born in a multicultural classroom, 2017.

One Friday Mr. B. sat down next to me and said, "What do you think you and I go to the Career Center and fill out a college application?" I stared back, then I looked at my homework. Could I get accepted to a university? Could I pay for tuition?

"I am not good enough," I replied.

"I want you to apply to Boise State University," said Mr. B.

"It is here in Boise, so you don't have to travel far from your family. Think about this. You have the whole weekend to think about it."

I nodded. My heart jumped. The bell rang, shaking me out of my negative thoughts. Soon I was taking the SAT and ACT college entrance exams and filling out applications. With help from the TRIO program [federal financial aid and encouragement for first generation college applicants] I entered Boise State as a freshman in the fall of 2003.

You are now well-settled in Boise. Where does the story go from here?

I am Bosnian-American. By sharing my story I am reclaiming my identity. I am healing. But not everything can be told in writing. Some experiences can only be felt. "Refugee," for me and many others, is more than a word. It is memory and experience. Often that experience makes refugees, if given the chance, eager to contribute. Education for me was the key to integration. I was silent. Education gave me voice.

In May I completed my doctoral degree in education. My calling is to teach others how to work with minority students, how to help them find their voice. I want to pay that forward. I've come this far because of people who cared and pushed me to reach ever-higher. People believed in me when I struggled to believe in myself.

BELMA SADIKOVIC, ED.D., teaches education at Boise State University and the College of Western Idaho. A specialist in teaching multicultural education and English as a second language, she is a co-founder of the Boise State Refugee Alliance.

9 | A Wider Perspective

Three lives – Eritrean, Bhutanese, and Afghan – help Boise see itself.

By Aileen Hale with Kathleen Rubinow Hodges

Fear of others, psychologists say, can be realistic or symbolic: viscerally real when rivals battle for scarce resources or culturally symbolic when rooted in stereotypes. Symbolic prejudice is more benign say researchers. An Idaho public opinion survey, recently published, suggests that prejudice can quickly dissolve when strangers become neighbors. "Those who live around and come into contact with refugees tend to hold more tolerant views," writes Jeffrey Lyons of Boise State University, a researcher who co-authored the study. In the southwestern part of the state where most refugees have resettled, poll respondents were the most likely to report positive feelings toward refugees.

The stories of Awot Haile of Eritrea, Ratna Subba of Bhutan, and Yasmin Aguilar of Afghanistan illustrate the process through which outsiders become insiders, breaking Idaho stereotypes. All crossed continents and cultures to start over in Boise. All give the city a more global perspective, revealing what Boiseans take for granted, helping us see ourselves. Their stories – traumatic, resilient, courageous – remind us that prejudice is hard to sustain when stereotyping gives way to compassion and doors open from within.

Awot Haile, Entrepreneur

Born in 1980 in a small town in Eritrea, Awot Haile can remember the devastation of war, the struggle to survive on the streets of Asmara, and life in a mud brick hut in a crowded refugee camp. Today, married and the father of three children, he owns a taxi business in the city of Boise and looks forward to a stable future. In January of this year, he related his story to Aileen Hale.

Many in his family fought Ethiopian troops for Eritrea's independence. The fighting was mostly in the countryside, but sometimes it came to the city. In 1990 when he was just 10 years old, a bomb killed Haile's mother, and the family broke apart. His father fled with one of his sisters; another sister joined the army; and his youngest brother

Olive leaves encircle a camel in the emblem of Eritrea.

Previous page: Awot Haile prepares lunch in a restaurant kitchen, Boise, 2013.

went to live with their grandmother. Only one sister stayed with Haile. Together, the two children went to Asmara, the capital city, to find work. Haile found a job lifting heavy containers of feed for animals until a falling container crushed his leg. Badly injured, he could not afford to see a doctor, so he used traditional medicine for a month. When he was finally able to go back to work, he realized that he would never play soccer again – a sport he had loved playing with his friends. To this day, he still uses a brace on his leg, although he is so agile you would never know, and he never complains.

In 1991 when Haile was 11 years old, his country won its independence from Ethiopia following a United Nations-sponsored referendum. "For many years there was peace, and there were no more bombs!" Haile exclaimed. People rebuilt their country and lived simply and happily. Everyone wanted a good future. Young people were finally able to return to school. Haile loved school. He said, "Going to school was one of the most wonderful times for me."

However in 1998 fighting began again along the Ethiopian border. Because Ethiopia had approximately 83 million people while Eritrea had only 4.5 million, many Eritrean citizens had to fight to build up their army. The government started to draft students. Anyone who was 17 years old was obligated to join the army.

Around the same time Haile's dad passed away from a disease. Haile remembers his father as a wonderful man with a big, kind smile – a friend to all who knew him. Everyone said Haile's smile was like his father's. When his father died, Haile's stepmother was pregnant. Six months after giving birth, she also died.

Now Haile was faced with the additional challenge of taking care of his new baby half-sister, as well as his other sister. There were no good jobs even though he took any work he could get to make money for his family. His baby sister was always ill because she had no baby formula or mother's milk. She would never recover. At the age of 10, she had the mind of a 2-year-old.

Haile continued working and taking care of his two little sisters alone for four years. Then the government told him that he must join the army. He went to them and showed them his still-painful injured leg, explaining that he needed a brace to walk. The government didn't care as they desperately needed men to fight, so they still made him serve.

Knowing he couldn't survive military life, he left everyone and everything without telling anyone, not even his sisters. He fled his city and took a bus to the border. He walked for hours, with his painful injured leg, to reach Ethiopia. Here he became a refugee, living with 10,000 others in a refugee camp. The people built their own houses with bricks from the soil and roofs made from grass. He survived in that camp for six years by making and selling his own bread.

Eritreans find shelter and relative safety across the Eithopian border in a UN refugee camp, 2012.

Finally he got the opportunity to legally resettle in America, and his friends held a big party to say goodbye. He flew from the capital of Ethiopia to Frankfurt, Germany, and then to Boise, Idaho. Like most refugees, Haile could not choose where he would be resettled. He was asked during his interview if he wanted to join relatives anywhere in the U.S., but he had none here. He arrived in Boise on June 30, 2010.

Haile likes Boise because it is a small city with very thoughtful people. Even so, the first eight months were scary

A WIDER PERSPECTIVE   141

for him. He had to quickly adjust to the language, culture, food, people and weather. He missed his family and had no one here to share his experiences or life with. He spoke no English. Yet he felt very supported by Boiseans, especially one man, Mike, who was his tutor. Mike helped him drive around town to get to know Boise; he taught Haile how to shop and how to prepare and eat American food.

Create Common Good, a Boise nonprofit, provides food service training for refugees and the underprivileged.

Haile started to learn English through classes at the College of Western Idaho. The International Rescue Committee assigned a specialist to help him find his first job. He entered an English and work skills training program run by Create Common Good (CCG), a nonprofit. He participated in English classes for one month at the downtown YMCA where he made friends with teachers (including this author, Aileen Hale) and tutors. As he quickly acquired a solid foundation in English, he moved on to practical work skills training where he studied industrial cleaning and customer service. He practiced English by talking with YMCA clients.

In collaboration with CCG, the Idaho Department of Labor provided paid opportunities for refugees to get hands-on job training experience for 90 days. Haile received culinary training under an internationally renowned chef, Brent Southcombe. Afterward CCG hired Haile at $7.50/hour. He started with CCG in 2011 and worked with them for three years as an assistant to the chef.

In addition to his work with CCG, he was also working three other jobs – at the Boise Fry Company, Joe's Crab Shack, and Cafe Rio – and so was able to acquire a lot of kitchen experience. In December 2013 Haile quit CCG. The organization had started as a nonprofit but shifted to becoming a for-profit production company. This organizational shift was difficult for him as rules and structures changed. He decided to start his own business as a taxi driver.

It was a good move. He is now the independent owner of Premium Cab Company and says he is very happy working with the people of Boise. He has felt a lot of support as he improved his English language skills and moved from one step to another in his jobs. He hopes to open his own store or maybe a gas station. He says: "God knows what I will open, but I have dreams to open my own business in Boise. I've been here six years, and within that time I've been very blessed by God. God has blessed me with a wonderful wife, Selamawit, in May 2011 and now with three beautiful children."

Haile's taxi service, 2017.

Haile arrived in Boise six months before his wife. They had been in a refugee camp together in Ethiopia for six years. When she first came to the U.S., she arrived in Columbus, Ohio. They arranged for her to move to Boise, where they got married in the courthouse. In June 2013 with help from Habitat for Humanity, they were able to buy a home. Haile is thankful that he and his family are living comfortable and stable lives.

Aside from the challenge of getting used to the cold weather, Haile and his family are happy in Boise. He feels the people are friendly, and the city is safe without much crime. He finds it a good place to raise his kids. His son has started in a Head Start preschool and is learning how to be hard-working and respectful. As he has never been to any other states, he can't compare what life would be like elsewhere. He came directly from Africa to Boise and has not left! He survived initial culture shock. Haile successfully passed the American citizenship exam in English and became an American citizen on December 17, 2015.

As a taxi driver, Haile meets a lot of people daily and finds the majority to be very nice. He says: "What helped me to love Boise was my work with Create Common Good. It showed me how the community helps each other. I've seen how CCG trained refugees and how people from the community volunteered to help with language and transportation until refugees were able to get their own means of transportation and work. I remember one American lady who helped an Ethiopian woman, giving her rides and tutoring her. I haven't felt much discrimination. I have seen refugees open stores in the International Market, and when it burned down, many people from the community donated money to help rebuild. For example, a friend of mine got help with re-opening his restaurant within three months. So I can say Boiseans really help refugees."

Haile has been in Boise for six years and says he hopes to live here a long time. He has aspirations to get his GED and then go to college. He has been able to accomplish more than many native-born Americans. Beginning with next to nothing, he has always been rich in spirit, tenacity, and compassion for others. To this day, with the salary of a taxi driver, he helps sustain the livelihood of numerous family members who remain in Eritrea and Sudan.

A snow leopard fronts the Himalayas in this postage stamp from Bhutan, 1966.

Ratna Hang Subba, Chef

Ratna Hang Subba, owner of the food truck Darjeeling Momo, is a stocky, outgoing, smiling man. It might seem on the surface that he doesn't have much to smile about. He was born in 1985 in Bhutan but fled from that country with his mother and sisters in 1992 when he was just 7 years old. Like many other Bhutanese, he lived for almost 20 years in refugee camps in Nepal. In February 2017 he invited author Kathleen Rubinow Hodges to his house for a conversation.

Subba's group, ethnic Nepalis (or Lhotshampa), had lived in Bhutan since the early 1900s when the British encouraged their Hindu ancestors to settle uncultivated lands. In the 1980s the Bhutanese government changed its definition of citizenship to exclude many Lhotshampas and began requiring national adoption of the Buddhist majority's language and dress. Lhotshampas campaigned for increased political and cultural rights. When the Bhutanese government took harsh measures in reprisal, over 80,000 fled, ending up in United Nations-supervised camps in Nepal. For the next 20 years, the Bhutanese government adamantly refused to allow their return, and they were not allowed to settle in Nepal.

Left: Ratna Hang Subba sells momo from his food truck.

Right: Momo are Tibetan-style dumplings filled with meat or vegetables and Nepalese spices.

This is Ratna Subba's story. He was born in Patalay village, Tsirang province, Bhutan. His father, a leader in the district, was threatened with arrest by the government and had already escaped to Nepal when Subba left with his mother and two younger sisters. He said: "We lost everything: land, home, society. It was a very sad moment." The mother and children ran out into the night and lived in the forest for two days without eating or drinking. Then, "somebody gave us a little food, and some other very good people showed us the way to India." They stayed in a shelter in Assam state for 15 days as a guest in someone's tent. He remembers his mother crying. They continued west into eastern Nepal. They had to beg for food. Others on the same journey died or became sick.

A WIDER PERSPECTIVE

Plastic tarps and bamboo shelter Bhutanese at Beldangi Camp in Nepal, 2014.

The family stayed first at a camp called Midar Surunga in the sand on the windy, dusty banks of the Mai Khola River. After six months, the office of the United Nations High Commissioner for Refugees (UNHCR) visited and brought tents, food (rice and oil), and even provided some school. A year later they moved a bit further west to another UNHCR camp called Beldangi, near the town of Damak, where they stayed for 19 years until 2012. At Beldangi there were 33,000 refugees living in rows of huts made of bamboo covered by plastic tarps. The huts were grouped into sectors, the sectors grouped into units, and the units had leaders. Despite the organization, Subba described the place as "lack of good food, lack of everything." They were not supposed to leave the camp. The Nepalese didn't like the refugees. Subba explained, "They hate us, they harassed us, they disrespect us."

Finally in 2006 an international agreement was brokered, and as Subba put it, "The government of America opened the door." The agreement paved the way for resettlement of the Lhotshampa in third countries with the U.S. agreeing to accept the largest number of people. Subba explained that United States officials came to visit the camp and "found we are the good person and qualify to come [to America]." His parents came to Boise first; then on November 8, 2012, Subba and his wife arrived in the city. As of early 2017 over 108,000 Nepali Bhutanese had emigrated, most to the United States. Only about 10,000 remained in the camps.

Within three months of his arrival in Boise, Subba had found a job as a chef because he already had seven years work experience as a cook in Nepal. Even though it had been illegal to leave Beldangi camp to work, he did. He explained "Refugee life is a hopeless life. I accepted Jesus, got hope, and decided to work as a cook." In Idaho he began cooking for Momo Dumplings restaurant in Meridian. However, the owners of that restaurant went back to Nepal to assist family after the earthquake of 2015. With help from other family members, Subba bought a food truck. He parks it at events in the spring, summer, and fall, and posts the locations on his Facebook page. He also works at a care center at nights. "I like helping people," he says.

He and his wife, Martha Rai, have three children. Three-year-old Josh, their youngest son, was born in Boise. Both his parents and hers share their home. The family wants to buy a house for themselves, and they are on the list for help from Habitat for Humanity. In the meantime, they live in a tidy rental in a west Boise neighborhood. Subba, his wife, his parents, and several other relatives all belong to a small Bhutanese Christian church and meet regularly for prayer. His goals in life are helping people, sharing God, being happy, and working with his food truck. His life, as he described it, has been an immense struggle. Statistics show a higher than average prevalence of anxiety and suicide for Bhutanese in the United States. However, at least on the surface, Subba is resolutely cheerful and forward-looking. And as this author can testify, he makes great dumplings!

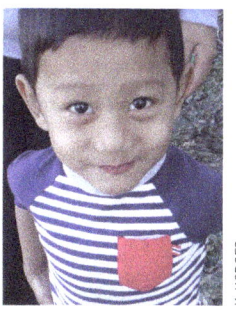

Boise-born Josh Subba, age 3, beams for the camera, 2017.

Yasmin Aguilar at the Agency for New Americans, 2015.

Yasmin Aguilar, Outreach Coordinator

In 2000 Yasmin Aguilar traveled alone to Boise, arriving as a refugee through the Agency for New Americans (ANA). She had been a doctor in her native Afghanistan, where she grew up in a well-educated family. She learned English when she was in high school, studied medicine in the Czech Republic, and completed a medical residency in gynecology and orthopedics. Though she was comfortable with English when she arrived here, adjusting to Boise was still a shock. She is now a community outreach coordinator at the Agency for New Americans. In 2016 she recounted her journey to author Aileen Hale.

In 1992 the Northern Alliance, an extremist Muslim faction, gained the upper hand in Afghanistan's ongoing civil war. They attacked her family's house because her father had been in the air force. At the same time the atmosphere had become unsafe for women. The family fled to Pakistan. There, Aguilar completed her medical studies.

In 1996 she got a job with an American-based organization, Mercy Corps. She worked in refugee camps addressing the topic of women's health, which was sensitive

Northern Alliance troops in Mazar-e Sharif, 2001.

and difficult for most people to talk about. Her biggest accomplishment was to set up health committees in order to give classes. She taught people the basics about their bodies, the prevention of disease, and birth control. She taught women about safe childbirth, immunizations for children, and basic sanitation. In the camps there was often no water or electricity, so she had to be resourceful.

During this time she and her family were forced to move back and forth between Afghanistan and Pakistan, as neither country was safe. Aguilar's public health work put her life at risk. "There were people not happy with a woman in power in the community, so I was attacked and kidnapped a few times."

Aguilar finally decided that to save her life, she had to leave. She was the only one in her family who was offered refugee status. Her office told her she could do whatever she wanted later, but in that moment it was her choice to save her life. It was extremely hard, but she knew it was the only way she could survive. When she heard she was going to Boise, Idaho, neither she nor any of her friends had the vaguest idea where it was!

Interviewed by the *Boise Weekly* in October 2009, Aguilar explained that in the U.S. she could not practice medicine without going back to school and getting recertified, but she had to support her family back in Pakistan financially. She thought, "OK, there are already many hospitals with intelligent doctors, but as a social worker in this field, I could help many refugees." She still misses medicine, but supporting refugee resettlement in Boise has been a fulfilling second career.

The transition was difficult. She explained that "one of the hardest parts of being a refugee is losing your identity, people not knowing who you are: your background, your education, or anything." When she would explain where she was from, people would say, "Poor you!" They reacted to her with sympathy but very little understanding and with a lot of stereotyping. She thought to herself, "People just see what the media says and have very little information about the true situation of the people of Afghanistan." Because she knew English, people assumed she understood everything; yet she still had to learn basics like where the bus stop was, how to get around town, and where to shop. Because of her black hair, many spoke Spanish to her.

An Afghan woman defies the Taliban in the 2014 documentary *Playing With Fire*.

"People were not educated enough, asking me weird questions," she said. For example, she was asked many times if she had been raped. She responded by asking how they would feel if they were asked the same question. However, she is hopeful that Americans will become more educated about the cultures that are integrating into their communities. Boise in particular is much safer than many other U.S. cities – very welcoming and friendly.

Aguilar is Muslim, although she does not cover her head or go to the mosque unless there is a funeral or some celebration. In Afghanistan, women never go to the mosque but instead practice their faith at home. Misperceptions about Muslims can be daunting. She has had people say to her face: "You don't belong here. You are a Muslim. Go back to your country." In spite of those negative experiences, she says, "The principle of America is to allow people to come and be free."

She has been living in Boise since 2000. Although she didn't choose her destination, at least it is safe. She joked, "So I came to a place like Boise. I think I'm happy. I'm still here for 16 years!" Her education allowed her to get a job two months after her arrival, and she has worked for the same agency ever since. She was able to buy a home soon after she arrived; this was a huge achievement for her, because in Afghanistan homes are usually in the names of men only. Aguilar met her husband, an electrical engineer from Mexico, when he started volunteering at ANA. She is now happily married and has learned to speak Spanish in addition to her other languages.

When people ask her where she's from, she says, "I'm from Idaho."

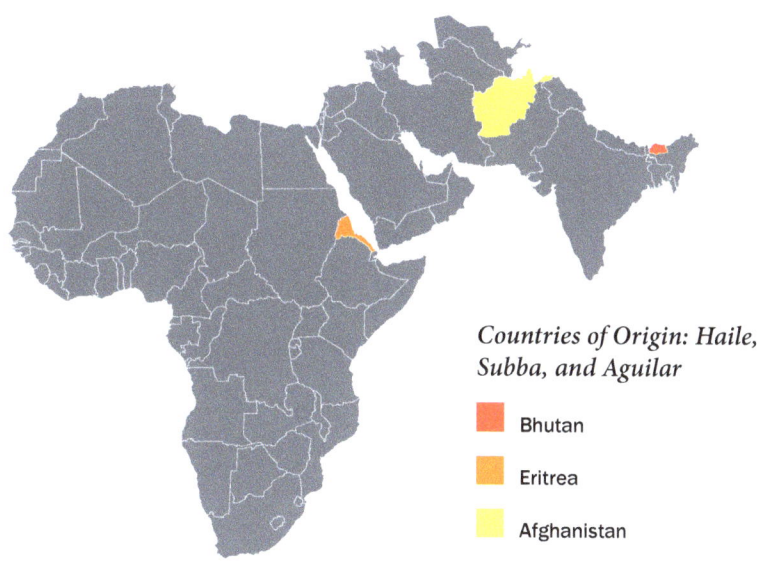

Countries of Origin: Haile, Subba, and Aguilar

- Bhutan
- Eritrea
- Afghanistan

AILEEN HALE, ED.D., holds a doctorate in international education from the University of San Francisco. A professor of education, she has taught at Boise State, Northwest Nazarene, and universities in Belize, Ecuador, and Indonesia.

Verse: *Always Home*

By Zoey Hills and Paw Kee Lar

My home is a place where moist thick air fills my lungs,
As the rain leaks through our wooden roof.
It is a place where the teachers leave burning red prints
On your skin with a bamboo stick
When you disobey the rules that keep you protected
From the outside world.

My home is a place where the men in green come take my safety.
It is a place where my village goes down in dark flames,
and turns into my past.

I walk from the place that kept me warm with laughter of those around me.
I run from the place I called home,
The place where my memories and childhood is stored.
I leave the place where my friendship lays
With the abandoned volleyball.
I leave my responsibilities of the household,
Of the pots and pans I would cook the family tradition in.

I come to a place where I sit in the dirt and watch
The hunger around me eat people alive.
I live in the dirty camp where children's stomachs
Are just full enough
That they don't starve,
And the taste of Thailand swirls around me
Until I give it the thing it so desires,
The feel of home.

I leave the camp where I was raised,
But never thought of as home.
I fly from the camps that healed my deep wounds,
And my thoughts
That tortured me.

I come to a place where I don't lose anyone,
Where only good thoughts come to mind.
I live in America,
But it is not the home that kept me warm and happy.
It is the home that keeps me safe.

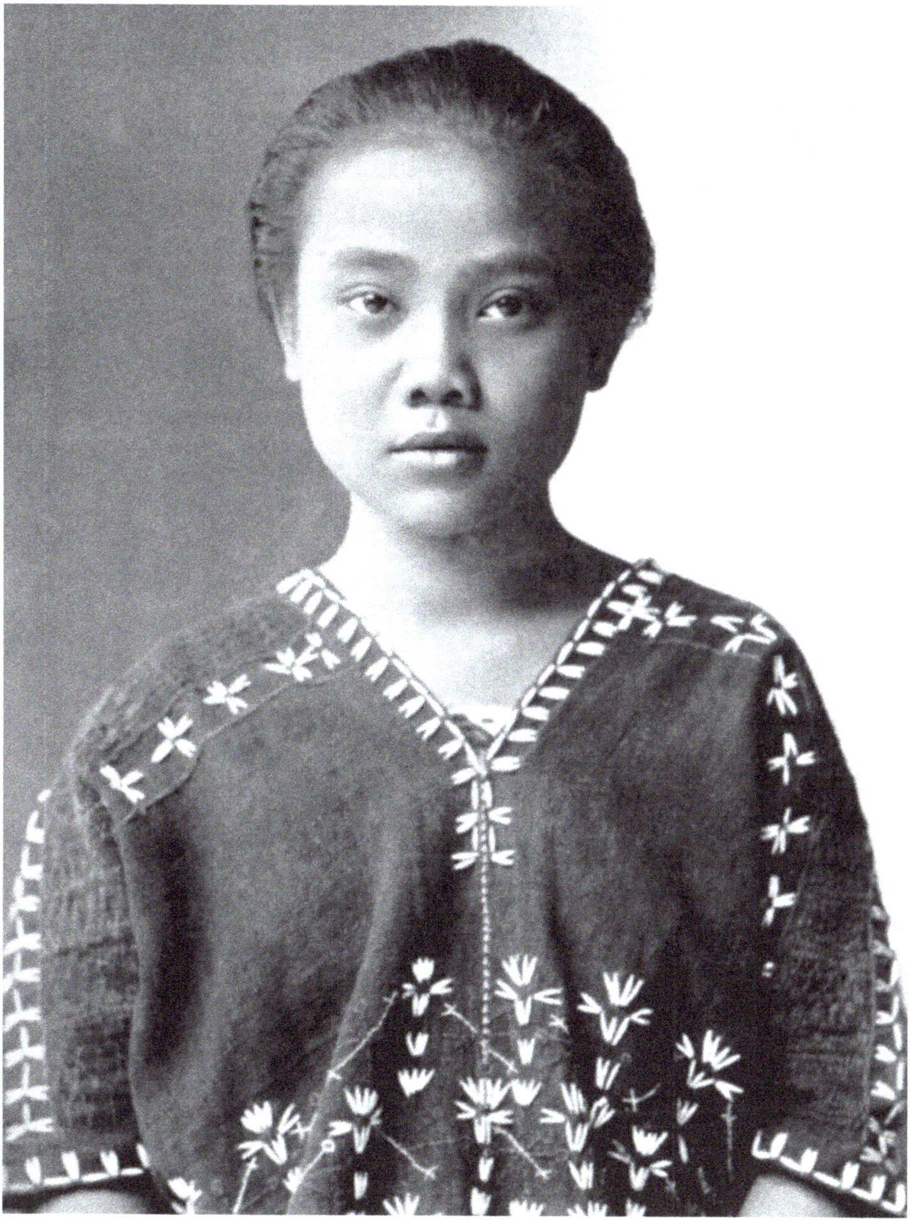

CUSTOMS OF THE WORLD

A Karen women in traditional dress.

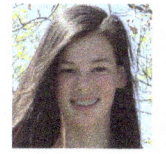

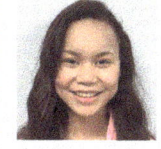

From *Nyumbani Means Home: A Collection of Collaborative Poetry* (2015).

ZOEY HILLS, left, is a 9th grader at Boise Junior High.

PAW KEE LAR is a Burmese Karen refugee from a UN camp in Thailand.

10 | A Matter of Trust

Teachers help refugees cope.

By Kathleen Mullen

Fifth-grader Malik said to her teacher, "I don't know how we have bones inside our body."

Her classmate Musa responded, "If you didn't, you'd be like this," and walked really wobbly, like a jellyfish.

Seizing the moment, teacher Suzanne Tyler, prompted, "If you didn't, Musa, what would happen if you didn't have bones inside your body?" Musa did the jellyfish walk again, and all the kids giggled.

They talked for a few minutes about bones and then Malik asked, "Does the bones inside us, does the face look scary?" Tyler pulled up a picture of a human skeleton on the classroom smartboard. Malik's eyes widened with new understanding. "Is that how our head's like inside? Ewwww!"

Malik's "ewwww" moment will probably seem unremarkable to most, but it reflected years of teacher effort, learning how to build trust among children who often had good reason to be distrustful. It took place in a classroom of refugee-background English Language Learners at Grant Elementary School in Boise. While names have been changed to protect student privacy, the learning curve faced by both students and school staff is real.

Tyler and her colleagues anticipated that most refugee-background students would be new to English but gradually realized that these children also needed time to feel safe in their surroundings in order to learn. As she explained, "The adults haven't always been trustworthy that they've been around outside their family, and so the students are oftentimes leery of any new adult." She continued: "These kids will shut down if they feel confronted in any way. They'll just shut down or fight back. ... So, it's much better to form a relationship with them. If they trust you, they'll work very hard for you."

In the spring of 2008 district administrators tasked Grant staff with developing a program for refugee English Language Learners in order to alleviate over-enrollments at neighboring schools. They recruited educators known for working hard to build a

positive school community; holding students to high academic standards; and supporting families facing serious challenges such as food insecurity, homelessness, lack of health care, and other basic concerns. The principal, Susanne Weeks, drew on this foundation as staff prepared over the spring and summer for the refugee students who would join their school in the fall.

The district provided support on curriculum and contact information for translators. They gave school staff as much information as possible on students' prior education, home language, and migration histories, although details were often scarce. Based on this information, the two fifth-grade teachers worked with their classes to produce a school newsletter about the new students' home countries. Weeks, Tyler, and other staff

A refugee child from Iraq shares a drawing with his teacher, 2016.

Previous page: Bhutanese cousins, granted asylum, hug and laugh for the camera after years in a refugee camp in Nepal, 2015.

visited the homes of students who would join the school in the fall, delivering to each a translated packet that included a welcome letter, information about the school, staff photos and names, and a collage depicting school activities and services. They also put together a two-week summer camp to help incoming students get to know some existing students and become familiar with school routines.

As the school year started and the newcomers began arriving, teachers quickly learned not to assume any particular kind of background knowledge. Many refugee youth spoke several languages but not English. Some came from former British colonies and brought strong verbal English but in colonial dialects with slightly different vocabularies. Some had been able to consistently attend school and thus arrived with native language literacy and a foundation in core academic subjects. Others arrived with severely interrupted or no prior schooling and lacked foundational literacy and academic skills. Many, like Malik, lacked background knowledge common to their native-born peers. Teachers also learned that refugee children were unfamiliar with activities common in American schools, such as coloring, doing puzzles, using a dictionary, checking out a library book, or using a computer to complete an assignment. Experienced at adapting lessons on the spot – a skill essential to good teaching – Grant staff found that working with refugee students brought a whole new dimension to thinking on your feet.

A Syrian child clings to a bag of raincoats and thermal blankets in a UN refugee camp.

"There's just no normal," said Tyler. "There's always different experiences. It's very unpredictable. Every day is unpredictable."

A sixth-grade teacher echoed this sentiment: "You have to be very flexible. Whatever you get hit with that day, just bend and go."

Beyond academics, staff encountered student behaviors they did not initially understand. Refugee students sometimes pushed others aside when waiting in line for food or school supplies or tried to hoard. Some became very withdrawn while others became physically aggressive. Some had trouble getting along with adults or fought with other students. As they came to know their teachers better, many children shared harrowing personal experiences: extended flight through hazardous jungle, separation from parents, witnessing the murder of a family member, escape from a mass killing, or other significant trauma. "So, we'll be in the middle of a lesson," Tyler explained, "and a student just might say, 'My brother was shot when he was holding me.' And it really took me a while to get used to that." She adds: "The traumatic stories have been a big, big challenge for me personally. … I've gone home and cried. … The more I hear about it, it doesn't shock me anymore. And it's the stuff you see in the movies. These kids have lived it."

Holistic programs for elementary education emphasize emotional health and community collaboration.

Detail from a child's drawing showing a plane bombing a village, 2014.

Tyler and others at Grant were not new to working with students who faced trauma or whose families had no safety net. They had worked for years, through endless grant applications and volunteer outreach, to connect families to supporting services. They learned to recognize domestic violence, parental drug abuse or incarceration, homelessness, a lack of medical and dental care, and gaps in meeting other basic needs. The social worker and school psychologist both split their time among multiple schools, but teachers could draw on them for guidance when available. For many, however, the experiences shared by their refugee students were qualitatively different and thus made supportive school relationships that much more important. "I always share with the teachers that these students don't automatically come with respect," said Tyler. "You need to earn their respect, and that's because of their past experiences."

Teachers understood that children learned best when not hungry, sick, or fearful. However, the task of serving as both educator and community support for their students, native-born and refugee, lay beyond the school's core educational mandate, and the task was sometimes overwhelming. Most responded by evaluating and adjusting their teaching practice, but some focused instead on perceived student deficits, criticizing refugee children and their families for not conforming to expectations.

The impetus to blame was familiar to principal Weeks, a 30-year veteran of public schools. She had for decades heard this type of complaint about lots of families across multiple schools, and she pushed back: "So, I hear too often, 'These kids [have] moved into our school and changed it. And basically they've lowered our scores.' No, we haven't adapted to figure out what these kids need. So it's more about schools need to learn to adapt and change. And change is difficult." Teachers at Grant found that developing an understanding of a range of migration contexts experienced by their students was an important first step. With the notion that difficult changes can be made a bit easier when informed by the experiences of others, the teachers and families presented here shared their stories in the hope of shortening the learning curve for others working to help launch all students toward bright futures.

Malik, Iraq

Malik, her father, mother, and two younger brothers arrived from Iraq. A straight-A student in her home country, Malik understood very little English when she first came to Idaho. "Like, when I went to my, the first school, the first day there was a boy speaking to me, and I was just like this [she sits up very straight, very still, and with wide eyes]. I didn't even understand what he's speaking." Despite arriving from a country that experienced multiple wars in recent decades, economic embargo, government collapse, and the rise of armed militias, her parents managed to consistently send her

Worldwide, only 50 percent of refugee children attend primary school.

to school until they left for the U.S. near the end of her third-grade year. Iraq once enjoyed a robust educational system; but by the time Malik started her formal education, many buildings had sustained significant damage and schools faced severe shortages of desks, chalkboards, chalk, texts, and other essentials. Malik's mother, Aasma, disliked her daughter's school, describing it as dirty and crowded with four children sharing a desk and teachers pressuring students to buy school lunch rather than bring food from home. Malik, however, enjoyed school and studied many of the same subjects as her

American peers except for physical education and science. She also attended special classes on Iraqi culture and learned in all-girl classrooms with only female teachers.

Malik shared stories that highlighted how larger events showed up in her daily life, explaining, for example, that police conducted regular house inspections in her neighborhood: "They come and they check your houses if you have a gun or something. We don't have, so they check everything. Last time they took a people they were sleeping, and they took the door and then saw a gun there. So they took them to jail 'cause they think they might kill people. But they don't. So they took them to jail, and after a while they took them out." She also matter-

Refugee counselors work hard to counter prejudice against Muslim girls wearing traditional clothing and scarves.

of-factly shared memories of someone setting fire to the house of a family friend and of a violent assault on a classmate. The wars in her country scattered relatives, sending aunts, uncles, and cousins across Europe and the Middle East.

Malik's father worked for Iraq's state utility agency, but government instability led him to leave his job and open a small bakery. He later worked for the American military, and the family eventually underwent a yearlong application process for refugee status. After notification that they would receive asylum in the U.S., they sold their home and made preparations to leave, only to be told that a mix-up meant they would not be going. Suddenly homeless, the family looked for a new place to live and spent another year sorting out their resettlement application.

Bilingual in Arabic and English, Malik's father found work in Idaho as an interpreter. It paid well enough that he could afford to move the family out of the shabby apartment in which they were originally settled and into a nicer one. The new apartment complex also housed a community center that offered homework help and after-school activities. With his educational background, Malik's father could help her with homework and with developing competence in both Arabic and English. Her mother did not yet speak English but helped her to continue using Arabic.

Malik was an eager student but initially did not like school in Idaho. She attended a different elementary school before coming to Grant and was one of only a few girls who dressed according to traditional Muslim understandings of modesty, or hijab. She covered her hair and did not wear short sleeve shirts, short skirts, or form-fitting clothes. Aasma said that other Iraqi students who chose a more western style of dress made fun of her daughter's appearance. "Because she wears scarf, she has no friends. Because she has the scarf, nobody likes to play with her. … Another people from Iraq, they tell her something not good about she wears scarf, not the people from America."

The teasing escalated to the point that Malik stopped wanting to go to school, but things changed when she transferred to Grant Elementary. "A lot of people were wearing hijab like me, and so I became friends with them," Malik explained. The teachers were nicer, too. "Here, if you do something not right the teachers will help you. … In my old [American] school, a couple of them were, like, mean."

To be successful in her new country, Malik thought she should, "be responsible, show respect, be honest." Her goal was

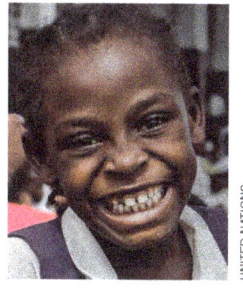

"When I grow up I want to be a doctor and help my family," says an eight-year-old refugee girl during her school presentation, 2014.

to go to college and start looking for a job so she could help her family. She thought she might like to work in medicine, perhaps in pediatrics, family medicine, or medical translation. Aasma viewed education as important for her daughter's future but did not know what Malik would need to do to reach her goals, explaining, "I have no idea about the education here." She worried that the fact that English was not Malik's native language would be an obstacle. The family received some guidance through Grant's college and career awareness program, which included visits to the nearby high school, local universities and technical schools, job shadowing, and other activities. The program gave Malik an idea of what comes after elementary school and how her future education links to her current aspirations. She and her family are still learning how to navigate life in a new country, however, and will likely need continued guidance as she works to pursue her goals.

So Min, Burma, Thailand

So Min, his mother, father, grandfather, and three siblings arrived from Mae La refugee camp in Thailand, the largest and oldest of nine camps along the Burma-Thailand border. So Min's family was resettled in Idaho during his first-grade year; but as a result of multiple family moves, he attended three different elementary schools before transferring to Grant during third grade. Generally quiet, he could be surprisingly chatty with his friend Musa in Tyler's fifth-grade English Language Learner class. Both boys loved sports and were on the basketball and track teams. So Min enjoyed sports but said he disliked it when students got too competitive. "Kids fighting over stuff. … They say, 'You're out. You're not supposed to.' Like that." Not entirely comfortable at his prior schools, he felt accepted at Grant. "They know me," he explained. "I'm most nervous asking people, 'Can I be your friend?' I don't really do that."

So Min's family is ethnic Karen, one of several minority groups in Burma that have sought some degree of self-rule since at least World War II. Historically Karen people fled into Thailand in response to fighting and returned to Burma when conditions allowed. The temporary nature of Karen displacement started to change in the mid-1980s, when the army began to intensify its military campaigns against minority communities and later refused to acknowledge the 1990 democratic election of Aung San Suu Kyi. Daily life in Burma came to involve seizures of food, livestock, and property; forced portering, mine-sweeping, or infrastructure construction; interrogation, torture, and killings; as well as the relocation of villages to government-controlled areas or their entire destruction. Seeking to extend its control, the army also employed detention without charges, incommunicado detention, imprisonment in life-threatening conditions, human trafficking, recruitment of child soldiers, and systematic rape.

Six decades of war have displaced hundreds of thousands of Burmese people from southeast Burma. Pictured: Mae La Refugee Camp.

So Min's parents fled to Thailand around the early 1990s, and he and his younger siblings were born and grew up in exile. The Thai response to Karen asylum-seekers vacillated over the years due to the large number of other refugees already in the country, attacks within Thailand by the Burmese military and Karen militias, and Thailand's political interests. Over the decades, government officials allowed families like So Min's to cross into Thailand or barred their entry; ignored or deported them; allowed them to establish camps within

Relief agencies provide a daily lunch to more than 33,000 Karen children in refugee nursery schools, 2012.

certain areas; offered refugee status to those in camps but not those living in Thailand outside camps; or offered money to return to Burma, a form of coercion that violated international principles.

When speaking of life at Mae La, So Min's older brother explained: "In there, in the camps, there's a lot of people in a small place. A lot of people. So, it's dirty there. And benefits, we don't have a lot of benefits." Researchers found that camp rations met short-term nutritional requirements but did not offer the balanced diet needed for long-term subsistence. Residents could grow vegetables and raise chickens or pigs, but space was limited, and restrictions on movement made it difficult to forage for supplemental food in nearby forests. Those with a source of income could buy extra food at small camp shops, but overall, there were micronutrient deficiencies among residents and a high prevalence of low weight and stunting among children.

So Min's father, Eh Mahn, was trained as a traditional weaver but faced limited job opportunities in Mae La. "We were poor," he said through an interpreter. "Kids come home, they want to do something but can't do nothing. In the refugee camp, we have no work." Those seeking work often had to venture beyond camp boundaries, although the Thai government technically prohibited it. This tenuous legal status left the Karen vulnerable to employers unwilling to pay minimum wage and to bribe demands or assault from government officials. Women and girls, in particular, faced abuse by humanitarian workers and Thai soldiers as well as exploitation in the Thai sex trade.

The decades-long conflict in Burma and prolonged exile in Thailand severely constrained Eh Mahn's educational opportunities – he could neither read nor write in his native Karen and did not know English – but upon resettlement, he found work busing tables. Glad to leave behind the imposed unemployment of the refugee camp, he enjoyed the ability to provide basic necessities for his family. His interpreter explained, "In here, if he want to buy something [with] his own money, he can buy. He can buy 'cause he have work."

Eh Mahn also valued the greater educational opportunities afforded to So Min in the U.S. "It's a good thing. Better education … when he grows up. School is good 'cause he can do more things."

So Min arrived in the United States before developing foundational native language literacy or any comprehension of English. He thus sometimes struggled with both languages. He spoke in English with his brothers, friends, and teachers but did not always know the words he needed to express himself. He spoke Karen with his parents but sometimes found it difficult to understand them. "When they just talk to me regular I understand every word. But sometimes, when they talk in a hard way … if you being silly or goofy, … it's not clear they using it in a different way. It's kind of hard." His efforts may have been complicated by the fact that his parents spoke two different Karen dialects.

So Min was not always able to finish class assignments on time, but Grant served lots of students who struggled to complete work at grade level, both native-born and refugee, and teachers extended deadlines when needed. "Sometimes I get all my work done. And my teacher sometime let me have

U.S. Refugee Arrivals, 2015

- 12% SOMALIA
- 18% IRAQ
- 26% BURMA (MYANMAR)
- 44% OTHER

a break, and then I get all my stuff done and I turn it in." With homework, So Min said, "I struggle a lot." He occasionally joined Grant's homework clubs before school or in the afternoon, but the school bus sometimes arrived too late or left too early for him to participate. When asked whether he had somebody who could help him, he replied: "Usually my grandpa. He showed me a lot of division stuff." He added: "Sometimes he's not at home, and then I have to figure it out myself, but I just do it. And then, if I get it wrong, then I come back at school and then I fix it with my teacher." Grant teachers could often be seen working with students between bells, during their own lunchtimes, and before and after school.

Asked how to be successful and have a good life in the U.S., So Min said: "Try to be respectful. Get all of your work done on time. [Learn] how to read, how to speak English." He used to want to be a scientist but recently decided he would really like to be a mechanic. He loves working with his hands and developed a strong interest in race cars. His parents encouraged him to work hard in school, and his father viewed education as a source of future opportunity. Yet researchers note that language minority students who lack first language literacy are likely to have to work doubly hard to learn academic content in English. This, combined with his homework struggles and his family's unfamiliarity with how to prepare for life after high school, highlights the importance of the guidance and support offered through programs at Grant Elementary.

> *"Try to be respectful. Get all of your work done on time. [Learn] how to read, how to speak English."*

Celeste, Burundi, Zaire/Democratic Republic of Congo, Tanzania

A year older than Malik and So Min, Celeste arrived with her parents and five siblings from a refugee camp in Tanzania around the beginning of third grade. She enjoyed the "fun stuff" at Grant Elementary, like math, music, PE, and going to the library. She helped Swahili-speaking newcomers navigate the uncertainties of life at a new school, translating assignments or showing them how to get lunch in the cafeteria, and demonstrated a sense of humor with her peers. When one student wandered around the classroom continually pestering others during group work time, Celeste said to her, "You need to put some glue on your bottom so you will stay in your seat." A sixth-grader, she worked at a third-grade reading level; but her teachers described her as a motivated student, and she felt confident in her abilities, explaining, "Now I know a lot of stuff, more than I knew in Africa."

Celeste grew up in Tanzania, but her father, Nyionzima, was originally from the tiny East African country of Burundi. He fled Burundi in 1972 when, in response to attacks by Hutu insurgents, the Tutsi-led government retaliated against the entire Hutu population, killing an estimated 200,000 people.

Refugees from Rwanda trek to a UN camp in Burundi, 2015.

He then lived in Zaire (now the Democratic Republic of Congo) for over 20 years under the kleptocratic and dictatorial regime of Mobutu Sésé Seko until events of the 1994 Rwandan genocide spilled over the border. In a little more than 100 days, 800,000 Rwandans, mostly Tutsi, were killed and thousands more were raped, tortured, or maimed. More than two million people, mostly Hutu, were displaced and more than one million people flooded into Zaire in just 48 hours. Mobutu

Zoera Daouda, 10, with her teacher in Djabal Refugee Camp, Chad.

provided protection and arms to leaders responsible for the genocide, who then intimidated or killed refugees. Laurent Kabila ousted Mobutu in 1997, largely helped by Rwanda and Uganda, and renamed Zaire the DRC. Regional tensions continued, however, and escalated into what would later be called Africa's First World War. The war officially ended via a 2002 peace accord, but several smaller military conflicts continued, and by 2003 regional fighting generated a death toll larger than World War II. Nyionzima and others living in Zaire/the DRC during the decade following the Rwandan genocide experienced government collapse, food shortages, malnutrition, massacres, rape, displacement, and increases in infectious disease, including AIDS and HIV.

Around the late 1990s, Nyionzima and his family escaped to Tanzania, a country that had for decades been a major refuge. At the time of the Rwandan genocide, Tanzania already housed hundreds of thousands of refugees from earlier conflicts, and the sudden massive influx from Rwanda overwhelmed both the government and international aid agencies. Hutus who had committed atrocities in Rwanda streamed into the country. Former leaders re-established political and military structures in the camps as part of efforts to win back power. They continued anti-Tutsi violence within the camps, creating a general climate of fear through theft, disruption of food distribution, intimidation, rape, and murder. Camp security presented such a challenge that by 1996 the United Nations supported efforts by the Tanzanian government to forcibly repatriate refugees, a move that contrasted starkly to the organization's long history of opposition to coercive return. Tanzanian soldiers and police pushed hundreds of thousands back across the border during 1996, 1999, and 2001.

Against this backdrop of massive social instability, Celeste's parents kept their family together. Nyionzima had worked as a farmer in Burundi and a fisherman in the DRC, but earned his living as a small-scale merchant in Tanzania. He never had the opportunity to attend school, though he tried to read and write a little bit in his native Kirundi. Celeste was born in Tanzania and grew up speaking Swahili rather than her parents' native Kirundi. Her father asked an uncle to teach her Kirundi after camp school each day so she could maintain her family language. Nyionzima described Celeste's schooling in Tanzania as difficult because camp aid agencies provided instruction only in French. Through an interpreter, he said, "I knew some kids they spend, like, five years in school but they don't speak well French." He said Celeste did not like school in Tanzania, found it difficult to learn in French, and repeated first grade because she failed the required end-of-grade test.

In Idaho, however, he described Celeste as a good student and wanted Grant staff to know he appreciated their work. "Everything they do for the kids is great job. I like it and I say thanks. May God bless you." He hoped Celeste would go to college. "I see if she continue her education, she will have a better life, because this world now, if you are not educated it's difficult. But if you are educated, you will have a better life." His limited formal education and lack of English skills prevented him from providing concrete assistance with schoolwork, but he supported Celeste by encouraging her to do her best. "My role is just to remind her every time to read the books, to know English, because English is the key of everything. Because if you know English, the school will be easy for you."

Though Nyionzima described Celeste as a good student and said she liked school, he noted that she sometimes did not like schoolwork. "When she get a big book, she say, 'That's too big for me. I can't read this because there is so many information. … Maybe if it is smaller, I can read it. But the big ones, I don't like it.'" Celeste, like So Min, lacked a solid foundation in a first language, and this complicated her efforts to develop competence in academic English.

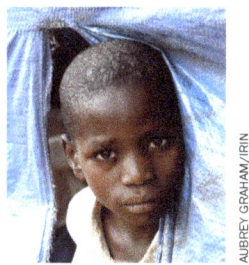

A student pokes his head through a tear in the tarp that walls his classroom in a Congolese refugee camp, 2009.

Tyler described Celeste's situation this way: "She can do grade-level work, but any assessment that people give her, they're going to think that she is much, much lower than she is. She thinks that, too. … She just needs somebody to spend time reading with her. That's what she needs. We have had tutors for her in the past, [but] people get busy. I mean, over the past few years, we've had a couple of different volunteer tutors work with her both at school and outside of school. And it just fell through. And the more [students] that we get, the more need.

Refugee students in the Bridge Program at Boise's Hillside Junior High, 2016.

Just managing all that is hard. … She's really within the normal range of development for somebody who's not literate in her first language. … She did not have a dominant first language."

Celeste participated in the school's program for students reading below grade level and sometimes attended the homework club offered before school. Teachers provided extra time and tutoring when needed, often at lunch or outside of standard teaching hours. Nyionzima explained that Celeste's older siblings sometimes helped but most had their own assignments to complete and faced the same language hurdles. Celeste, despite her challenges with academic English, possessed strong verbal skills and spoke only English with her sisters. She used Swahili with classmates from the same language background. With her parents, she used Kirundi and a smattering of Swahili.

Celeste was unsure about what kind of work she might like to do when she got older but knew that she wanted to continue her education. To do well in the U.S., she believed she must, "go to school so you can know more English, find a job, and go to college … [because] school makes people know more stuff, because if you don't know anything, you can't help yourself." She participated in school field trips, to the local community college, the local hospital for job shadowing, and other places so was developing a sense of future opportunities. However, working as she was to catch up to grade level, and with her family lacking experience with the American educational system, school-based programs and services would continue to be important to Celeste as she worked toward her goals.

Learning Trust

Malik, So Min, and Celeste each left their home country under different circumstances, experienced varying durations of displacement, and encountered disparate opportunities to stay safe and healthy and to gain knowledge and skills for the future. Each, however, experienced state destabilization and a rise in military conflict that led to the targeting of civilians and community structures. Malik's family fled state collapse and intense sectarian conflict. So Min and Celeste's families fled countries in which the government deliberately and systematically targeted members of their ethnic group with a wide range of human rights abuses. Celeste's family also fled profound communal violence and faced multiple displacements. All left countries in which children could not always trust adults; and school, when available, was not always safe. In coming to Grant Elementary, Malik and the others learned that they were safe at school, that teachers would help them develop the skills they needed, and that the school could be an important resource for struggling families.

In working with refugee students, Grant staff came to recognize that the combined experiences of missed schooling and prolonged insecurity meant positive school relationships were essential for refugee students' academic success. They learned that trust served as a foundation for student development and that it was enhanced when students felt safe, respected, and supported. Though staff sometimes felt overwhelmed by the dual tasks of teaching and helping families patch their safety nets, they hoped that their experiences could help inform efforts in other communities.

Ethnicity of Boise District Limited English Students

- 42% HISPANIC OR LATINO
- 20% BLACK/AFRICAN AMERICAN
- 19% ASIAN/PACIFIC ISLANDER
- 17% WHITE
- 3% OTHER

KATHLEEN MULLEN, M.A., is a Boise-based consultant specializing in healthy schools and refugee education. She holds a masters in education from Boise State University.

Epilogue: *Hysteria challenges a city's commitment to human rights.*

By Errol D. Jones

From Pakistan to North Africa across the horn of the Muslim world, the ravages of war have unleashed an unprecedented refugee crisis. It has shaken the United States at a vulnerable juncture between paranoia and the rule of law.

Muslims, especially, have been targeted by the politics of exclusion. In 2015 in response to President Barack Obama's plan to admit more Syrian refugees, Idaho's Butch Otter was one of 28 governors to call for a moratorium. "It makes no sense under the best of circumstances," said Otter, who denounced Syrian refugees as "people who have the avowed desire to harm our communities."

A moratorium on refugee resettlement, Otter believed, would keep Idaho safe by giving Congress time to strengthen the vetting process. Refugee advocates responded by pointing to the testimony of U.S. security experts. Homeland Security and immigration officials maintained that refugee vetting, already extreme, was more deliberately thorough and multi-layered than any other immigration process the United States had ever invented. Advocates worried that a moratorium would endanger refugees at a time when the United States, for humanitarian reasons, needed to double down on its moral leadership of the free world and increase its quotas.

In April 2016, nevertheless, Idaho Republicans passed a House bill – blocked in the Senate – to prohibit Idaho courts from acquiescing to Islamic or Sharia law. The Legislature, citing the "Muslim agenda," also rejected an international treaty for the protection of children. Idaho became the only state to reject the treaty, but the vote was reversed a few months later when it appeared that the state might have disqualified itself from a federal appropriation.

Two months later right-wing bloggers were fanning the flames. *Breitbart News*, *The Drudge Report*, and *Refugee Resettlement Watch* fictionalized a report about an assault on a child at a Twin Falls apartment complex. Police had acknowledged an incident involving a 5-year-old girl and two older boys – one from the Sudan, the other Iraqi. It was not a rape, but because all participants were juveniles, the records were sealed.

REFUGEES WELCOME IN IDAHO

EPILOGUE

Left: Thirteen stars encircle Idaho in the emblem of the Three Percenters, who want to ban refugees.

Right: Protesters face off in Boise, 2016.

Previous page: Boiseans rally at the Idaho Statehouse in support of refugee resettlement, 2015.

Bloggers immediately embellished the story with the false accusation that Syrian refugees had raped the girl at knifepoint. Bloggers then published the rumor that Obama was punishing Idaho by sending the Syrian hordes.

Outspoken among the resistance were "militiamen" calling themselves the Three Percent of Idaho. In June 2015 they had rallied against refugees at the College of Southern Idaho Refugee Center. They wanted the center closed, and the militiamen also strongly supported passage of federal legislation to do two things already done: grant Homeland Security power to approve refugee admissions, and compile a list of refugees on public assistance.

In November 2015 about 100 militiamen and sympathizers rallied at the Idaho Statehouse. Brandon Curtiss, president of the militia, and spokesman Chris McIntire proclaimed their core beliefs. First was the conviction that Islam was a political organization bent on world domination; second, that the federal government had been complicit in fostering the destruction of Christian traditions. America, said the Three Percenters, had become unrecognizable; Muslims, an existential threat. "The guys just can't believe how many Muslims there are in the country today," said journalist Shane Bauer who went undercover to report on militias in a story for

Left: Rally and a counter protest, Boise, 2015.

Right: Welcoming refugees at the Boise airport, 2017.

Mother Jones. Bauer reported waterboarding and the use of Tasers. Meals were prepared with bacon grease to expose Muslim infiltrators.

Other critics were more concerned about the perceived financial burden of the refugee resettlement program. The blog *Refugee Resettlement Watch*, based in Maryland, damned the Obama administration for financing a corrupt "industry" of resettlement programs. Unwittingly, bloggers alleged, the U.S. taxpayers were footing the bill for "a self-perpetuating global enterprise." Relief agencies had been staffed by "hundreds of taxpayer-supported U.S. contractors [who] are largely refugees or immigrants." Their sinister purpose was "to gain entry for more refugees, usually for their co-ethnics."

Refugee advocates claim that refugee vetting is vigilant. They point out that no refugee in the history of the program, which began with the Refugee Act of 1980, has committed an act of terror in Idaho. In 2016, nevertheless, a federal jury convicted an Uzbekistan national for terror-related crimes. Fazliddin Kurbanov, age 33, a truck driver living in Boise, had been admitted seven years before with refugee status. He was sentenced to 25 years for aiding Uzbek jihadists in his home country and possessing the makings of a homemade bomb.

Refugee advocates remained undeterred. Religious groups welcomed refugees; fellowshipped with them; and donated food, clothing, and household items. Restaurant patrons and many employers valued the rich diversity refugees brought to the whitest American state west of the continental divide. In Twin Falls and Boise, where the dairy industry struggles with a labor shortage, refugee workers are welcome in the production of milk, yogurt, and cheese. "If a refugee has a job, they are no longer a refugee," said yogurt tycoon Hamdi Ulukaya, founder of Chobani LLC, whose largest plant is in Twin Falls. Immigrants and refugees comprise about a third of his factory workforce.

A refugee from Bhutan, resettled in Boise, milks cows at an Oregon dairy, 2009.

"We need to take time to understand one another," says Bob Schmidt, who drives a van for the Twin Falls Refugee Center. Schmidt, age 61, has tried but failed to convince his own brother and some of his neighbors that people who shovel barns deserve some respect. "How many people do you know that would get up every day, on time, for a job where a cow might take a s--t on them?" The people Schmidt drives to work "do it again, day after day." He's never heard a complaint.

"We're all children of refugees, immigrants, in some form or fashion," said Chris Talkington, Twin Falls councilman and former mayor. Like Schmidt, he saw the storm of hatred that hurt everyone in Twin Falls. "Does our economic vitality get put up on the shooting gallery for the sake of folks who'd like to ship [refugees and immigrants] away?"

An answer came seven months later from the candidate who had swept Twin Falls County with 66 percent of the vote. On January 27, 2017, President Donald Trump issued a sweeping decree: all refugee admissions would be suspended for 120 days until new processing measures were considered. Syrians were to be banned indefinitely. Annual refugee quotas would be reduced from 110,000 to 50,000. All immigration from Iraq, Iran, Libya, Sudan, Somalia, Yemen, and Syria would be suspended for 90 days and, after that, allowed to enter only on a case-by-case basis.

"It was a punch in the gut," said David Lubell of Welcoming America who denounced the executive order. Lubell, age 40, tall, bearded, and earnest, addressed an overflow crowd at the opening plenary of the 2017 Idaho Conference on Refugees held on the campus of Boise State University. The speaker condemned Trump's decree as a "societal deviation from our core values." Compassion had been superseded by fear.

Statehouse rally for refugees, 2015.

Horrified but optimistic, advocates seized the teachable moment to urge Boiseans to do even more. "It takes something bad to start something good," said Lubell. Boise had become an "amazing model" of a welcoming city. Boise institutions had rejected the politics of exclusion. Whether other Idahoans would overcome the cycle of xenophobia remained to be seen.

 **ERROL D. JONES, PH.D.**, is professor emeritus at Boise State University. He is the winner of the city's biennial award for excellence in civic contributions to history and the arts.

Credits

Special thanks to Allan Ansell, Amanda Ashley, Jill Bail, Lynde Bailey, Corey Cook, Roy Cuellar, Jim Duran, Kara Fink, Slobodanka Hodzic, Joe Jaszewski, Megan Jones, Jason Lantz, Allyson Maynard, Tina Nguyen, Jan Reeves, Kelly Roberts, Nancy Tacke, Maria Tellez, and Tara Wolfson. Applause, also, for Bruce and Laura DeLaney who appreciate that there are no great cities without groovy bookstores downtown.

Selected Sources

Alvarez, Priscilla. "What Should the U.S. Do About Refugee Resettlement?" *Atlantic*, March 29, 2016.

Anker, Deborah E. "The Forty Year Crisis: A Legislative History of the Refugee Act of 1980." *San Diego Law Review* (1981): 9-89.

Anne, Wallace Allen. "A Word With Jan Reeves, Director of the Idaho Office of Refugees." *Idaho Business Review*, June 13, 2016.

Bain, James. "Ancient Grain Sparks Adventure." *Toronto Star*, January 9, 2002.

Baker, Richard P. "Eastern European Refugees: Implications for Social Work." *Journal of Sociology and Social Welfare* 16 (September 1989): 81-94.

Bates, Karen Grigsby. "Nailing the American Dream, With Polish." *All Things Considered*, National Public Radio, June 14, 2012.

Bauer, Shane. "Undercover With a Border Militia." *Mother Jones*, November/December, 2016.

Bauman, Stephan, Matthew Soerens, and Issam Smeir. *Seeking Refuge: On the Shores of the Global Refugee Crisis*. Baltimore: World Relief, 2016.

Bhabha, Jacqueline. *Child Migration and Human Rights in a Global Age*. Princeton: Princeton University Press, 2014.

Blau, Francine D. and Christopher Mackie, eds. *The Economic and Fiscal Consequences of Immigration*. Washington, D.C.: National Academies Press, 2016.

Boehm, Chelsee. "Community As Constant: Oral History and the Boise Police Department, 1990-2014." Masters project, Boise State University, 2017.

Bonner, Raymond. "Some Who Fled Rwanda Return as Zaire Opens Border Crossings." *New York Times*, July 25, 1994.

Brees, Inge. "Refugee Business: Strategies of Work on the Thai–Burma Border." *Journal of Refugee Studies* 21, no. 3 (2008): 380-397.

Bubb, Ryan, Michael Kremer, and David I. Levine. "The Economics of International Refugee Law." *Journal of Legal Studies* 40, no. 2 (2011): 367-404.

Chan, Sucheng, ed. *The Vietnamese American 1.5 Generation: Stories of War, Revolution, Flight, and New Beginnings*. Philadelphia: Temple University Press, 2006.

Chetail, Vincent. "Are Refugee Rights Human Rights? An Unorthodox Questioning of the Relations Between Refugee Law and Human Rights Law." In *Human Rights and Immigration*, edited by Ruth Rubio-Marín, 19-72. Oxford: Oxford University Press, 2014.

Cone, Devon. "The Process for Interviewing, Vetting, and Resettling Syrian Refugees in America Is Incredibly Long and Thorough." *Foreign Policy*, November 30, 2013.

Evans, Rosalind. "The Perils of Being a Borderland People: On the Lhotshampas of Bhutan." *Contemporary South Asia* 18 (March 2010): 25-42.

Fisher, Ian and Norimitsu Onishi. "Chaos in Congo: Many Armies Ravage Rich Land in the 'First World War' of Africa." *New York Times*, February 6, 2000.

Friedman, Francine. *Bosnia and Herzegovina: A Polity on the Brink*. London: Routledge 2004.

Gatrell, Peter. *The Making of the Modern Refugee*. Oxford: Oxford University Press, 2013.

Haines, David W. *Safe Haven? A History of Refugees in America*. Sterling, VA: Kumarian Press, 2010.

Harlan, Chico. "In Twin Falls, Idaho, Co-dependency of Whites and Immigrants Faces a Test." *Washington Post*,

Opposite: Abdullah Salman, center, a refugee from Iraq, graduates with the class of 2016 at Boise's Borah High.

Next Page: Sar Bah Bi came to Idaho from Burma in 2011. She and her husband, a refugee from Somalia, grow vegetables for sale at downtown Boise's Saturday market.

Selected Sources (continued)

November 17, 2016.

Hodges, Kathleen Rubinow. "A History of the Vietnamese Community in Boise, 1975-1990." Masters thesis, Boise State University, 1991.

Holley, Peter and Sarah Larimer. "I'm Looking at Drudge: 'Syrian Refugees Rape Little Girl at Knifepoint in Idaho' – All False." *Washington Post*. June, 23, 2016.

Johnson, Kirk. "Idaho City of Immigrants Debates Taking In Middle Eastern Refugees." *New York Times*, October 1, 2015.

Jones, Megan. "See How We Are: Voices of Refugees and Their Helpers During Resettlement." PhD diss., Boise State University, 2005.

Jordan, Miriam. "In Aftermath of Terror Attacks, Tensions Rise in Idaho Over Refugee Workers." *Wall Street Journal - Online Edition*, February 13, 2016.

Kelly, James Patrick. "What the Teff? An Ancient Grain Takes Hold in Southern Idaho." *Boise Weekly*, October 3, 2012.

Kenney, David Ngaruri and Philip D. Schrag. *Asylum Denied: A Refugee's Struggle for Safety in America*. Berkeley: University of California Press, 2009.

Kohrt, Brandon A., Sujen M. Maharjan, Damber Timsina, and James L. Griffith. "Applying Nepali Ethnopsychology to Psychotherapy for the Treatment of Mental Illness and Prevention of Suicide Among Bhutanese Refugees." *Annals of Anthropological Practice* 36 (2012): 88-112.

Kruesi, Kimberlee. "Boise's Refugee Resettlement Program Considered an International Success." *Salt Lake Tribune*, April 23, 2016.

Kyle, Zach. "Treasure Valley Employers Are Embracing Refugee Workers More Than Ever." *Idaho Statesman*, November 19, 2016.

Lorch, D. "Refugees Flee Into Tanzania From Rwanda." *New York Times*, May 1, 1994.

Malkki, Liisa. *Purity and Exile: Violence, Memory, and National Cosmology Among Hutu Refugees in Tanzania*. Chicago, IL: University of Chicago Press, 1995.

Michael, Tom. "What Are Immigrants Doing for Idaho's Economy?" Boise State Public Radio, February 21, 2017.

Minten, Bart, Seneshaw Tamru, Ermias Engida, and Tadesse Kuma. "Transforming Staple Food Value Chains in Africa: The Case of Teff in Ethiopia." *Journal of Development Studies* 52, no. 5 (May 2016): 627-645.

Mullen, Kathleen. "A Holistic Approach to Promoting Student Engagement: Case Studies of Six Refugee Students in Upper Elementary." Masters thesis, Boise State University, 2014.

Nshombo, Fidel Mwendambali. Route to Peace: *The Cries of the Forgotten Refugees in Deadly Camps*. Boise: Borderline Publishing, 2009.

Nshombo, Fidel Mwendambali. *Route to Peace 2: A Life for Lives*. Boise: Borderline Publishing, 2011.

O'Connor, Anahad. "Is Teff the New Super Grain?" *New York Times*, August 16, 2016.

St. John, Warren. *Outcasts United: An American Town, a Refugee Team, and One Woman's Quest to Make a Difference*. New York: Spiegel & Grau, 2009.

Sassoon, Joseph. *The Iraqi Refugees: The New Crisis in the Middle East*. London: I.B. Tauris, 2009.

Shephard, Ben. *The Long Road Home: The Aftermath of the Second World War*. New York: Anchor Books, 2012.

Skogly, Sigrun. *Beyond National Borders: States' Human Rights Obligations in International Cooperation*. Singapore: Intersentia, 2006.

Sowell, John. "Closed Boise Restaurant's Egg Rolls Still in Demand – And You Can Learn How to Make Them." *Idaho Statesman*, June 7, 2016.

Spooner, Samantha. "Very Soon Ethiopian Food Will Rule the World ... So Wash Your Hands and Get Set." *Mail and Guardian Africa*, November 16, 2014.

Taffesse, Alemayehu Seyoum, Paul Dorosh, and Sinafikeh Asrat. "Crop Production in Ethiopia: Regional Patterns and Trends." Ethiopian Development Research Institute, *Working Paper* 11 (2012).

Thrall, Trevor. "Let Syrian Refugees In – All of Them." *Atlantic*, October 21, 2015.

UNHCR. *Resettlement Handbook*. Rev. ed. October 2014.

United States General Accounting Office. "The Indochinese Exodus: A Humanitarian Dilemma." *Report to the Congress*. Washington DC: April 24, 1979.

Vaughn, Justin S., Jeffrey Lyons, and Matthew May. *Second Annual Idaho Public Policy Survey*. Boise: Boise State University School of Public Service, 2017.

Urban Studies and Community Development at Boise State University relates the past to the future of cities, their politics and economics, their environmental and cultural trends. Visit sps.boisestate.edu/urban/ or contact professor Amanda Ashley, program director, at AmandaAshley@boisestate.edu or (208) 426-2605.

BOISE STATE
UNIVERSITY

INGRAM PLACES THE
UPC CODE ON THIS
PAGE BY ITSELF

www.ingramcontent.com/pod-product-compliance
Lightning Source LLC
Chambersburg PA
CBHW040334300426
44113CB00021B/2748